Darryl Strawberry is an incred[...] whose personal transformatio[...] *Around* will fill you with hope because it is filled with godly counsel and life-changing truth that will truly turn your life around! Grand slam in every way!

JACK GRAHAM, *PASTOR OF PRESTONWOOD BAPTIST CHURCH AND POWERPOINT MINISTRIES*

Darryl Strawberry has an intimate understanding of God's redemptive power and his ability to change a person from the inside out. Over the years, I have watched Darryl become a bold and unapologetic preacher of the gospel of Jesus Christ. In his new book, *Turn Your Season Around*, Darryl shares not only how he has put Christ at the center of his life but also how you can experience God's abundant life for yourself.

ALBERT PUJOLS, *TWO-TIME WORLD SERIES CHAMPION, THREE-TIME NATIONAL LEAGUE MVP, TEN-TIME MLB ALL-STAR*

Since I'm a fan of Darryl Strawberry, it broke my heart to learn about his personal struggles with drugs and other related problems. It was very encouraging to hear that he has become a Christian and has transformed his life! But how did it happen? How does someone go from an addict to an evangelist? In *Turn Your Season Around*, Strawberry describes what it takes to follow God every day. This biblically rich book will challenge you to walk more closely with Jesus and will remind you that God is always with you during all your trials, *no matter what.*

MARIANO RIVERA
FORMER CLOSING PITCHER FOR THE NEW YORK YANKEES
THREE-TIME DELIVERY MAN OF THE YEAR AWARD
FIVE-TIME AL ROLAIDS RELIEF MAN AWARD
THIRTEEN-TIME ALL-STAR
FIVE-TIME WORLD SERIES CHAMPION
FIRST PLAYER TO BE ELECTED UNANIMOUSLY INTO
THE BASEBALL HALL OF FAME (2019)

Some people tell us how to turn our lives around. Others show us how to turn our lives around. Darryl Strawberry powerfully does both with his own compelling story of authentic transformation. Every person searching for hope will be transformed by his inspiring real-life message.

GENE APPEL, SENIOR PASTOR OF EASTSIDE
CHRISTIAN CHURCH, ANAHEIM, CALIFORNIA

Many of us fell in love with Darryl Strawberry the baseball player, but the victories he's won off the field far surpass any ring or title that sporting competition can offer. Darryl's life is the epitome of turning one's season around.

TODD DULANEY, GRAMMY-NOMINATED
SINGER/SONGWRITER

This book is an absolute walk-off grand slam for the gospel by one of the greatest hitters who ever played the game, my friend Darryl Strawberry. Everyone who has played baseball will never view it the same. Those who've never played will grow to love it as Darryl leads us graciously and powerfully to love and live for Jesus! The Bible says, "Preach the word; be prepared in season and out of season; correct, rebuke and encourage—with great patience and careful instruction" (2 Timothy 4:2 NIV). Darryl does that, and no matter what season of life you find yourself in, he can help you turn it around. The first time I ever spoke to Darryl, he said, "Pastor, if you want me to come and talk about baseball, I don't want to do that. But if you want me to come and talk about Jesus, I'm your man." Every man in America, young and old, needs to read this book. You'll be changed by it and giving it away to everyone you know. It's a story that needs to be heard, from one of the humblest men I know.

BARRY L. CAMERON, PASTOR OF CROSSROADS
CHRISTIAN CHURCH, GRAND PRAIRIE, TEXAS

Darryl Strawberry had the sweetest left-handed home run swing in baseball, surpassed only by the sweetness he has in his heart for God and for people. He was a warrior on the diamond, and now he is a warrior in his mission to help transform lives as God has dynamically transformed his own. I'm honored to call Darryl a friend and a brother. I strongly encourage you to read his book. You will be both encouraged and blessed!

MICHAEL FRANZESE

Darryl's life is one of the most amazing examples of God's transformative power, comfort, and grace. He turned the most important season of his life around, and so can you.

ED MYLETT

My friend Darryl Strawberry is an inspiring example of a man who has a life-changing relationship with Jesus. It has been said that genuine faith does not make bad men better but rather dead men come to life! That is the transformation I see in Darryl, and you'll discover how that same power can change you if you read *Turn Your Season Around*.

CAM HUXFORD, LEAD PASTOR OF COMPASSION CHRISTIAN CHURCH, SAVANNAH, GEORGIA

The first time I heard Darryl Strawberry speak, sharing the principles in this book, I had forgotten he was a legendary baseball player. I was more captivated by the message of an anointed man of God. This book will show you how to move closer to God through his Word and the power of his Spirit. It is a must-read for those who love God.

TOMMY BARNETT, GLOBAL PASTOR OF DREAM CITY CHURCH, PHOENIX, COPASTOR OF LOS ANGELES DREAM CENTER

The split second of a ball exploding off a bat and hitting the winning home run in a World Series is the same amount of time that is needed for God to change and transform a human life. By reading this book, you will be mesmerized by the power of God to change a life for the better and for his glory.

DUDLEY RUTHERFORD, *PASTOR OF SHEPHERD CHURCH, PORTER RANCH, CALIFORNIA*

Turn Your Season Around describes how to stay the course and follow God no matter what you may have done and no matter what may have been done to you. God can change anyone's life. No one can tell this story better than Darryl Strawberry.

MILES McPHERSON, *PASTOR OF THE ROCK CHURCH, FORMER SAN DIEGO CHARGER, AND AUTHOR OF THE THIRD OPTION: HOPE FOR A RACIALLY DIVIDED NATION*

TURN YOUR
SEASON AROUND

TURN YOUR SEASON AROUND

HOW GOD TRANSFORMS YOUR LIFE

DARRYL STRAWBERRY

WITH LEE WEEKS

Z ZONDERVAN
BOOKS

ZONDERVAN BOOKS

Turn Your Season Around
Copyright © 2021 by Darryl Strawberry

Requests for information should be addressed to:
Zondervan, *3900 Sparks Dr. SE, Grand Rapids, Michigan 49546*

Zondervan titles may be purchased in bulk for educational, business, fundraising, or
sales promotional use. For information, please email SpecialMarkets@Zondervan.com.

ISBN 978-0-310-36086-5 (softcover)
ISBN 978-0-310-36088-9 (audio)
ISBN 978-0-310-36087-2 (ebook)

All Scripture quotations, unless otherwise indicated, are taken from the ESV® Bible
(The Holy Bible, English Standard Version®). Copyright © 2001 by Crossway,
a publishing ministry of Good News Publishers. Used by permission. All rights
reserved.

Scripture quotations marked CSB® are taken from the Christian Standard Bible®,
Copyright © 2017 by Holman Bible Publishers. Used by permission. Christian
Standard Bible®, and CSB®, are federally registered trademarks of Holman Bible
Publishers.

Scripture quotations marked NIV are taken from The Holy Bible, New International
Version®, NIV®. Copyright © 1973, 1978, 1984, 2011 by Biblica, Inc.® Used by
permission of Zondervan. All rights reserved worldwide. www.Zondervan.com. The
"NIV" and "New International Version" are trademarks registered in the United
States Patent and Trademark Office by Biblica, Inc.®

Scripture quotations marked NKJV are taken from the New King James Version®.
Copyright © 1982 by Thomas Nelson. Used by permission. All rights reserved.

Any internet addresses (websites, blogs, etc.) and telephone numbers in this book
are offered as a resource. They are not intended in any way to be or imply an
endorsement by Zondervan, nor does Zondervan vouch for the content of these sites
and numbers for the life of this book.

All rights reserved. No part of this publication may be reproduced, stored in
a retrieval system, or transmitted in any form or by any means—electronic,
mechanical, photocopy, recording, or any other—except for brief quotations in
printed reviews, without the prior permission of the publisher.

Cover design: Curt Diepenhorst
Cover photo: Skyler Julian / MEMORIES MEDIA
Interior design: Phoebe Wetherbee

Printed in the United States of America

21 22 23 PC/LSCH 10 9 8 7 6 5 4 3

This book is dedicated to my mother, Ruby, and my siblings, Michael, Ronnie, Regina, and Michelle. We wouldn't be who we are today, Mom, without your faith, strength, and love.

To my beautiful wife, Tracy. God used you to lead me back to him. I would not be the man I am today without you.

To our amazing children, D. J., Diamond, Jordan, Jade, Jewel, Alice, Omar, Austin, and Evan. I love each one of you so very much.

CONTENTS

FOREWORD

Most people know Darryl Strawberry as a sports legend. A baseball icon. A childhood hero. A model athlete. A world-famous success. The best of the best.

And rightly so. An amazing right fielder, Darryl played seventeen seasons of baseball for the Mets, the Dodgers, the Giants, and the Yankees. But it was in the batter's box that he won so much of his well-earned fame. Known for his prodigious and numerous home runs, Darryl never failed to please his abundant fans when he stepped up to the plate.

Darryl was an eight-time All-Star, four-time World Series champion, two-time Silver Slugger Award winner, 1983 National League Rookie of the Year, 1988 National League home run leader, and New York Mets Hall-of-Famer.

Over the course of Darryl's career, he batted two three-home-run games, batted .333 with two stolen bases and two runs in twelve All-Star at-bats, and hit two pinch-hit grand slams in the same season. Tall, strong, and confident, Darryl had an imposing presence and impressive reputation that shook rival teams.

But what many don't realize is that Darryl was a broken man—broken before he even started playing baseball. Underneath the swagger and success were a pain and a spiritual emptiness that fame, fortune, women, drugs, and the love of the game could never satiate. With more money coming in than most of us could dream of, Darryl found out that money doesn't bring happiness and in fact opened up doorways to even more problems and discontent in his life.

Darryl told me, "My pain led me to my greatness, but my greatness would eventually lead me to my destructive behavior." It was his destructive behavior that brought him to rock bottom and finally led him to the healing and salvation found in a relationship with Jesus Christ.

I first met Darryl Strawberry at the White House. At a meeting for evangelical leaders, the president opened up the podium to anyone who had something to say. Darryl made his way to the mic, and I was immediately struck by his boldness, his love for Jesus, and his down-to-earth humility.

I've invited Darryl to come and be interviewed in front of the congregation of the church that I pastor, as well as before forty-five thousand people in Angel Stadium for one of our Harvest Crusades.

Again I was impressed that no matter the question, Darryl brought the answer back to Scripture and used his life experience to point to God and give him glory. His love for Jesus is contagious, and his boldness is amazing!

With humility and candor, Darryl confesses, "I was a heathen, I was a liar, I was womanizer, I was a cheater, I was an alcoholic, I was a drug addict—but I was a sinner saved by grace. God's grace is sufficient. No matter who you are, he still has grace for you. No matter how far you go down, he still has a perfect plan for you."

That's the prevailing theme you'll find woven throughout this book and throughout Darryl's life and testimony: because of God's grace, it's never too late to "turn your season around."

Be prepared for yet another home run as you read this captivating book!

Greg Laurie, pastor and evangelist,
Harvest Ministries

ACKNOWLEDGMENTS

I dedicated this book to my mother, Ruby, my wife, Tracy, and the rest of my immediate family. But there's much more that needs to be said.

Mom, you molded our lives through your grand example of faith and nurtured them with your unconditional love. I have cried many tears, wishing you could see me now as the man I am today and whom you knew I would always become. You went home to the Lord with your unwavering faith in each one of us. I know this is why we are all saved and will spend eternity with you in heaven. I love you, Mom!

My wife, Tracy, has stayed, prayed, endured, and never stopped believing in me. The strength, love, and faith of my mother carried on through you! You are the love of my life, forever and always. I'm forever grateful for you and the life we live together as one.

To our children: I will never be able to find the words to describe all the emotions I have in my heart. From my deepest regrets, to our most precious and private memories, to the journey of healing we have all traveled together. You all are the light of my life, and I love each of you. Thank you for always loving me.

To Papa Leonard and Ma Leonard: I am beyond blessed to have had you as godparents for all these years, leading me, guiding me, and loving me through the good times and the bad. I love you with all my heart!

To Gerry and Peggy Boulware, my father- and mother-in-law, and to all my in-laws: It is hard to find the words to tell each one of you how much I love you. You loved me, supported me, and accepted me at my very worst. You lifted me up and helped love me back to life.

To Pastor Jesse and Missy Quiroz and our Journey Church family: My wife and I are so grateful for having such a wonderful church family and pastoral leadership who have always accepted, loved, supported, and embraced every part of us as individuals, our family, and the work the Lord has called us to finish. We love you all so much!

To all my friends over the years: I'm forever grateful for all the amazing friendships from each one of you who have always been real in my life, loved me, and supported me! Love you guys!

I want to thank Andy Rogers, the entire Zondervan team, and Lee Weeks for always believing in me and the message God put in me. I'm forever grateful for the freedom you gave me to illustrate my story through the boldness of God's Word that I pray will transform many lives. Thank you for your hard work and dedication to this amazing book.

INTRODUCTION

I'm just a nobody trying to tell everybody
About Somebody who can save anybody.

Yͦͧou might not know that song. Though it has been adapted
by others, it was written by The Williams Brothers, a singing quartet that performed widely from the 1960s through the
1990s.

Those lyrics are the song of my heart.

For a season of my life, I was at the top of my game, and my
game was baseball. Mammoth home runs. Eight All-Star Games.
Four World Series rings.

But seasons change. Bad choices and other misfortunes
knocked me down, hard. And God began a process of teaching
me, reshaping me, and leading me into a new kind of life.

Sports often serve as metaphors for life. You know, like when
life throws a curve ball you weren't expecting that drops perfectly across the center of your world for strike three. We've all
been there. When your plans fail, your dreams are crushed, your
heart is broken, or your trust is betrayed, it feels like striking
out. Whether or not you've ever worn a uniform for athletic

competition, one thing is sure—if you're reading this book, then you're all in for this game called life. And like a baseball career, seasons of life come and go. King Solomon said it best in Ecclesiastes 3:1–8:

> For everything there is a season, and a time for every matter under heaven:
>
> > a time to be born, and a time to die;
> > a time to plant, and a time to pluck up what is planted;
> > a time to kill, and a time to heal;
> > a time to break down, and a time to build up;
> > a time to weep, and a time to laugh;
> > a time to mourn, and a time to dance;
> > a time to cast away stones, and a time to gather stones
> > together;
> > a time to embrace, and a time to refrain from embracing;
> > a time to seek, and a time to lose;
> > a time to keep, and a time to cast away;
> > a time to tear, and a time to sew;
> > a time to keep silence, and a time to speak;
> > a time to love, and a time to hate;
> > a time for war, and a time for peace.

I don't know what your current season of life looks like. But I do know this: the Creator knew before you were born that you would be where you are right now. And whether you are happy or sad, have plenty or are in want, are delighted or disillusioned, God's desire is that you experience his powerful presence every day of every season of your life. It doesn't matter whether life has you soaring or slumping, winning or losing—victory in Christ is possible. This I know because Jesus tells us so in John 16:33: "I have said these things to you, that in me you may have peace. In the world you will have tribulation. But take heart; I have overcome the world."

God can turn your season around for your good and his glory. He did it for me, and he can do it for you.

RECALIBRATION

You might ask, "How can I be an overcomer? How do I turn my season around?"

When I was struggling through a 3-for-30 hitting slump, my batting coach had me refocus my attention on the baseball by slowly tossing it so I could see my bat make contact with the baseball. It seems simplistic, perhaps even more Little League than major league, but it actually helped me sharpen the mechanics of my swing. By slowing my swinging motion, I was able to recalibrate the synchronized timing of dropping my front leg and turning my hands to rotate the bat.

Similarly, God allows us to go through seasons of change, uncertainty, or trials to slow us down so we can regain his perspective and acknowledge our dependence on him. As the psalmist writes in Psalm 46:10, "Be still, and know that I am God." Many people experience a healthy slowdown during a time of illness or injury. For example, how did you respond to the COVID-19 lockdown? When the world came to a crashing halt, did you take the opportunity to draw closer to God or perhaps reconsider your relationship with him?

I hope this book can be a helpful pause for you, a chance to get back to the basics, to recalibrate your relationship with God. Throughout these chapters, we are going to contemplate God's rescuing, redeeming, and restoring work in Jesus Christ—and the responses he wants from us. The apostle Paul prayed that his readers would "know the love of Christ that surpasses knowledge, that you may be filled with all the fullness of God." That is my prayer for you too. The apostle continues with a stunning benediction: "Now to him who is able to do far more abundantly than all that we ask or think, according to the power at work within us, to him be glory in the church and in Christ Jesus throughout all generations, forever and ever. Amen" (Ephesians 3:19–21).

These verses promise us realities beyond imagination—I call them God's RBIs. They are his rewards for those who are fully yielded to his plans and purposes. As you continue reading, you'll find nine faith-filled responses that produce life-changing results in the lives of Christians. God must become the center of our lives, and his ways should be the measure of everything we do. That's why there's so much Scripture quoted in these pages. It's the power of God's Word, and not my own, that will heal the deepest wounds and empower you to turn your season around.

So are you ready to receive, redefine, renew, reveal, release, reflect, reclaim, restore, and rejoice for your good and God's glory?

If so, it's *game on!*

RECEIVE GOD'S GRACE

> By grace you have been saved through faith. And
> this is not your own doing; it is the gift of God,
> not a result of works, so that no one may boast.
>
> ### EPHESIANS 2:8–9

I had everything but I had nothing.

As the 1983 National League Rookie of the Year and a perennial All-Star throughout that decade, I had fame and fortune. But I battled a lifelong identity crisis that controlled my heart and mind off the field, and that undermined my on-the-field performance. My thoughts and choices away from the ballpark's bright lights ultimately sabotaged my best intentions like an off-speed pitch to an overanxious batter.

Alcohol, drugs, partying, possessions, and promiscuity couldn't quench my hunger for acceptance, purpose, and peace.

My relentless pursuit of physical, mental, emotional, and sexual euphoria to mask the pain of my father's rejection provided short-lived diversions and only left me craving more. And with each foray into decadence, I sank deeper into depravity. It was like a cesspool of quicksand suffocating the life out of me.[1]

SELF-INDULGENCE NOW

Take my word for it: the Enemy, Satan, really does come "to steal and kill and destroy" (John 10:10). He is a liar and deceiver who always peddles worldly wisdom as counterfeit solutions to our problems. Satan's playbook hasn't changed since the serpent told Adam and Eve in the garden of Eden that they could be wise like God by eating the eye-pleasing fruit God said to avoid. And with Adam and Eve's disobedience, sin was unleashed on humanity.

I use SIN as an acronym for self-indulgence now. Every time we choose our way over God's way, we sin. It has been said that sin always takes us further than we need to go, keeps us longer than we want to stay, and costs us more than we can afford to pay.

Sin is costly. My sins cost me two failed marriages and millions of dollars in fines and penalties. Incarceration and multiple stints in rehab for cocaine addiction and alcoholism destroyed relationships and robbed me of years of peace and purpose. The Bible says in Romans 6:23, "The wages of sin is death," but the second part of that verse offers one of the most beautiful truths in Scripture. It changes our eternal fate like a walk-off home run that snatches victory from the jaws of defeat: "But the free gift of God is eternal life in Christ Jesus our Lord."

That free gift of God is his GRACE—God's riches at Christ's expense.

God's unmerited favor lavished on us through the sacrificial death of his Son, Jesus Christ, and his finished work on the cross is the only payment sufficient for the forgiveness of your and my sin debt. Ephesians 2:8–9 states, "By grace you have been saved through faith. And this is not your own doing; it is the gift of God, not a result of works, so that no one may boast." By God's grace and through the power of the Holy Spirit, I came to realize that my selfishly destructive choices and wicked ways offended God, who is perfect, holy, and righteous.

Sin always takes us further than we need to go, keeps us longer than we want to stay, and costs us more than we can afford to pay.

I wept uncontrollably each night while attending a weekend evangelistic crusade in Anaheim, California, in 1991. I should have been the happiest person on the planet, having recently signed a five-year, $20.25 million contract with my hometown team, the Los Angeles Dodgers—the second most lucrative contract in the history of Major League Baseball at the time. But in reality, I was miserable, empty and broken inside. An alcoholic and a womanizer, I was going through a painful divorce of my own doing.

At that crusade, I realized for the first time that my ability to hit majestic home runs and leave fans starstruck in my path couldn't make me right with God and free me from the bondage of sin. Human abilities can't bridge the gap that exists between the sinful human condition and God's glorious perfection. We can't achieve or buy a right relationship with God or perform godly works to make us good enough for God. God's standard is not good; his standard is perfection. But here's the good news—God did not leave us helpless and hopelessly alienated from him. He did not leave me in my pit of debauchery, strung out on cocaine, or abandon me when I was in jail for violating probation. When I was running from God, full throttle on my path of destruction, he pursued me relentlessly with his unconditional and unfailing love. First Corinthians 6:9–11 paints an accurate picture of my condition before and after receiving God's gift of grace and salvation in Jesus Christ: "Do you not know that the unrighteous will not inherit the kingdom of God? Do not be deceived: neither the sexually immoral, nor idolaters, nor adulterers, nor men who practice homosexuality, nor thieves, nor the greedy, nor drunkards, nor revilers, nor swindlers will inherit the kingdom of God. And such were some of you. But you were washed, you were sanctified, you were justified in the name of the Lord Jesus Christ and by the Spirit of our God."

"And such were some of you." That was me before I surrendered my life to Jesus and received him as my Savior and Lord. But when I placed my faith in Jesus, I underwent a spiritual heart transplant, effectively exchanging my selfish and sinful heart for his selfless and sinless heart. I was justified—made right with God—because my heart was replaced with his Son's heart.

I used to wonder why God didn't reject me after I repeatedly turned my back on him. Then I learned that God loved you and me before we had the capacity to love him. He has always loved us, even while were sinners. Romans 5:8 states it best: "God shows his love for us in that while we were still sinners, Christ died for us." I am overwhelmed by the reality that God loved me at my worst, in my most rebellious state. In the midst of my deepest and darkest sin, he continued to call me to himself—chasing me with his perfect love and not judgment. Jesus longed to heal me, not hurt me, and to deliver me, not punish me. I was on my way to hell as fast as I could get there. But God set up my detour. He never left me. I am amazed that God redeemed me from the punishment my sin demanded. God's perfect and sinless Son, Jesus Christ, died in my place through a cruel death on a cross. And I am still in awe that God has restored me to a thriving relationship with him through Jesus's resurrection from the grave. Because Jesus defeated sin and death, I too can live victoriously every day and for eternity.

THE BALL FIELD OF HUMANITY

You and I would never have experienced God's miracle of salvation without first receiving that which we couldn't earn or deserve—God's amazing grace. It is made available to us because

Jesus humbly came to us when we couldn't go to him. The apostle Paul provides us a great word picture for this in Philippians 2:5–8: "Jesus . . . though he was in the form of God, did not count equality with God a thing to be grasped, but emptied himself, by taking the form of a servant, being born in the likeness of men. And being found in human form, he humbled himself by becoming obedient to the point of death, even death on a cross."

This passage blows me away when I think about how God, who created heaven and earth as well as every human being on the planet, stepped onto the ball field of humanity and became one like us. He left his limitless uniform of majesty and glory in heaven and clothed himself in human flesh. But Jesus didn't come to earth as the number one draft pick and wasn't heralded as the next great phenom. Quite to the contrary, he was born among farm animals because there was no room for him anywhere else. His earthly father, Joseph, was a carpenter. Jesus's mother, Mary, endured whispers of promiscuity because she was pregnant and not married. Yet she had never been sexually intimate with Joseph. She was in fact a virgin. Instead of being escorted by legions of angels or golden chariots of fire, Jesus came to earth miraculously through the womb of a virgin. He grew up in a modest Jewish home and learned his father's trade. Even though he began teaching in the temple as a teenager, he continued to submit to the authority of his earthly parents. As Jesus grew in wisdom and stature, he did so within the limited confines of the human experience, all the while being God in the flesh. He lived and breathed among sinners, although he never sinned. He knew their thoughts and motives but judged them not. He made the blind see, the lame walk, the deaf hear, the mute speak, and the dead come to life. He cast out demons, healed lepers, and calmed the stormy seas with a command. He turned water to wine and fed thousands with only five loaves and two fish. The only truly innocent and guiltless person to ever live, Jesus was hung on a cross between two thieves. Taking your sin and my sin on himself, Jesus experienced hell's fury on our behalf when God the Father looked away as Jesus cried out, "My God, my God, why have you forsaken me?" When we wrap our heads and hearts around how Jesus came to earth on a rescue mission for sinners like you and me, it should humble us, causing us to turn from our sin and turn to God in thankful repentance and glorifying worship.

Jesus stands ready to meet you exactly where you are. When you turn from your ways and turn toward Jesus, he always stands ready to receive you just as you are. Don't make the mistake of thinking you have to clean yourself up or change your life before inviting Jesus into your life. Jesus can clean house better than Mr. Clean himself. We don't have to put on the shine or dress to impress to garner his attention or acceptance. You don't have to be fixed to be found by Jesus. He is not impressed with your uniform, what you drive, or where you live. Whether you have the corner office overlooking the city skyline, work behind a counter or in a cubicle, or wear a tool belt, Jesus is an equal opportunity deliverer. Whether you're in great physical health or chronically ill, he understands your suffering and fears better than you do. Nothing you do can make God love you more than he already does, and nothing you do can make him love you

You don't have to be fixed to be found by Jesus.

any less. Jesus paid your sin debt in full when Roman soldiers scourged, spat on, and beat him beyond recognition before nailing him to a cross. When Christ declared, "It is finished!" before taking his last breath, he was declaring that his atoning sacrifice alone makes it possible for you and me to have a right relationship with God.

You can know your Creator as your heavenly Father. Once you choose to give your life to Jesus Christ, you are saved by grace through faith in his finished work of the cross. Eternal victory over earthly suffering and evil will become your reality when Christ returns for his bride, the church. This is what the apostle Paul boldly declares in Romans 8:31–39. Slowly read this passage and meditate on God's promises:

> What then shall we say to these things? If God is for us, who can be against us? He who did not spare his own Son but gave him up for us all, how will he not also with him graciously give us all things? Who shall bring any charge against God's elect? It is God who justifies. Who is to condemn? Christ Jesus is the one who died—more than that, who was raised—who is at the right hand of God, who indeed is interceding for us. Who shall separate us from the love of Christ? Shall tribulation, or distress, or persecution, or famine, or nakedness, or danger, or sword? . . . No, in all these things we are more

than conquerors through him who loved us. For I am sure that neither death nor life, nor angels nor rulers, nor things present nor things to come, nor powers, nor height nor depth, nor anything else in all creation, will be able to separate us from the love of God in Christ Jesus our Lord.

Now that's what I call a guaranteed contract! But there is one condition. Did you see it at the end of verse 39? It states nothing will be able to separate us from the love of God *in Christ Jesus*. All the promises and assurances of God's miraculous love in the previous eight verses hinge on one's profession of faith in Jesus Christ. In other words, you can experience the life-changing, purpose-giving, way-making, wound-healing, vision-changing, freedom-unleashing love of God only by trusting in the finished work of Jesus on the cross for the forgiveness of your sins and the promise of eternal life. Jesus couldn't have said it any clearer than in John 14:6: "I am the way, and the truth, and the life. No one comes to the Father except through me."

THE STARTING AND FINISH LINE

In the game of baseball, home plate is ground zero for winning and losing. Just as Jesus is the only way to God, a baseball player can score only by safely crossing home plate. An irregular pentagon with two parallel sides, home plate is the measure by which the umpire calls strikes and balls. It's the starting and finish line for the batter or base runner who scores a run. To score, the batter must safely advance to a base ninety feet *away from* home plate, then proceed ninety feet two more times before safely returning home. It seems counterintuitive to go in the opposite direction of where you need to be, but that's the challenge. Like much of the base runner's path to home plate, in life I ran in the opposite direction of God's standard for right and wrong as a man, husband, and father. But as in baseball, when I ran toward home plate, victory became attainable. Similarly, when I quit running from Jesus and instead ran to him, then I discovered the Savior who wanted to heal me and not hurt me; claim me and not abandon me; and love me, lead me, and change me, not judge me.

So, I ask you, have you received God's gift of grace in Jesus's sinless substitutionary death on a cross and victorious resurrection from the grave? Have you invited him into your life by acknowledging that you're a sinner needing his forgiveness? If not, you can do so right now by praying something like this:

Dear God,

I have sinned against you by choosing my ways over your ways. Please forgive me for disobeying you. Please give me the faith to turn from my sinful ways and surrender control of my life to you. I believe Jesus Christ is your Son who died on the cross for my sins and you raised him to life three days later. I trust Jesus as my Savior and commit to following him as my Lord from this day forward. In Jesus's name I pray,
Amen.

If you made this commitment for the first time, the Bible says that angels in heaven are rejoicing over your decision. Praise the Lord and congratulations! You are a winner for all eternity—a trophy of God's grace. You've just experienced your first spiritual RBI—realities beyond imagination. But let me be clear, coming to faith in Christ does not immediately solve all your problems and cure all your ills. Yes, your eternity is secure in the hands of Jesus. He is holding on to you and will never let go. Jesus's shed blood on the cross and victorious resurrection from the grave have signed, sealed, and delivered your eternal fate. I like to say it this way: I'm covered by the blood of Jesus. It is as though God clothes us in his righteousness. Obviously, this is not by our own doing but exclusively by what Christ did for us.

Coming to faith in Christ does not immediately solve all your problems and cure all your ills.

Once God rescues you from the death penalty of your sin and redeems you for eternity, his restoration process is just beginning. He leads us through a process of becoming more like Jesus as we learn to trust him with our lives, follow his example, and obey his teaching.

TRUST THE PROCESS

In baseball, my minor league and major league coaches told me to "trust the process." I had to learn to adjust to the increasing speed of the game and deceptive craftiness of the pitchers as I advanced through the levels of minor league competition. With each advancement, the level of competition increased as players were bigger, faster, stronger, and more skilled. As I continued playing and working my way up through the minor league system, I learned to be a more disciplined hitter by refraining from swinging early and often at pitches out of the strike zone. As an outfielder, my instincts were sharpened as I gauged how to read the baseball as it came off the bat. In determining to run in or back to catch the ball, an outfielder has to quickly decide their first step. That split-second decision can make all the difference in catching the ball in the air, fielding it on the ground, or chasing it to the fence. When I made it to the big leagues with the New York Mets, I quickly realized "the process" would start all over again. Although I had arrived at the pinnacle of the baseball world, every game in a major league uniform demanded I make the necessary adjustments to gain a competitive advantage over my opponent.

Similarly, a Christ follower's development process involves making corrections, adjustments, and recommitments to how one thinks, speaks, and acts based on the principles of God's Word—the "owner's manual." Along my faith journey, I have experienced painful consequences for disobeying God as well as his grace and the blessings that follow obedience. As I have disciplined myself to spend more time studying God's Word, I've become more aware of the enemy's lies and deceitful tactics aimed at robbing me of the joy, peace, and purpose for which

God created me. Although my baseball career is over, I am a work in progress as God molds me into who he wants me to be for his glory, not mine.

Perhaps you received God's gift of grace through faith in Jesus Christ some time ago and sin keeps tripping you up. Turn from your wicked ways in repentance and come back home where you left your heavenly Father. Pray something like the psalmist David declared in Psalm 51:1–3 (CSB):

> Be gracious to me, God,
>   according to Your faithful love;
>   according to Your abundant compassion,
>   blot out my rebellion.
> Completely wash away my guilt
>   and cleanse me from my sin.
> For I am conscious of my rebellion,
>   and my sin is always before me.

The Bible describes King David as a man after God's own heart—not because he was perfect but because he sought God's forgiveness and reconciliation through repentance of his sin. When you truly repent of your sin, you agree with what God says about it. Sin in the eyes of a holy and righteous God is wickedness. To call it anything else—a mistake, a weakness, an accident, or an addiction—fails to acknowledge that when we sin, we sin against God. And compared with God's standard of righteousness and perfection, our sin is a wicked offense to a holy God. So call your sin what it is, and ask God to forgive you for sinning against him. Then move forward as a champion for Christ, just like the old hymn states: "Trust and obey, for there's no other way to be happy in Jesus but to trust and obey."

THINK ABOUT IT

1. In what ways have you been practicing self-indulgence now (SIN)?
2. Think of your life as a baseball diamond. At what times have you been running *away* from home? What's the best path for you around the bases and back to home plate?
3. What does *grace* mean to you?
4. Reread Ephesians 2:8–9. What does that tell you about your role in God's miraculous work of salvation?
5. Take another look at Philippians 2:6–8. How does it describe Jesus's behavior, and how do you feel about that?
6. What does God's development process look like in your life? How can you "trust the process"?
7. What do your daily decisions show about Jesus's importance to you?

2ND INNING

REDEFINE YOUR IDENTITY

I have been crucified with Christ. It is no longer I
who live, but Christ who lives in me. And the life
I now live in the flesh I live by faith in the Son
of God, who loved me and gave himself for me.

GALATIANS 2:20

When I donned the legendary pinstripes as a member of the New York Yankees in 1995, I joined a fraternity of World Champions unlike any other franchise in the history of professional sports. Twenty-three Major League Baseball Hall of Famers such as Babe Ruth, Joe DiMaggio, Mickey Mantle, Lou Gehrig, Whitey Ford, Yogi Berra, Reggie Jackson, Derek Jeter, and Mariano Rivera have helped lead this historic franchise to a Major League Baseball record of twenty-seven World Series titles—more than twice as many as any other professional baseball organization. I had the honor of wearing the Yankees logo on my cap and chest for three World Series championship seasons with the Bronx Bombers in 1996, '98, and '99 before retiring from the sport with my fourth World Series ring.

Near the end of my baseball career, just to be wanted by a multibillion-dollar organization known for sparing no expense to acquire the best baseball talent in the world sparked a resurgence in my production on the field after several subpar years with the Dodgers. In 1998 I hit twenty-four home runs in only 101 games with the Yankees, including two pinch-hit grand slams. But after every game, when I took off the pinstriped uniform in front of my clubhouse locker, the same empty feeling returned that had trolled me with the Mets, Dodgers, and Giants. Sadly, my whole identity was wrapped up in being a professional baseball player. My uniform was merely a facade for greatness, shielding the brokenness that ached within me.

STRIPES

Four years before I put on the Yankee pinstripes, I had claimed Jesus's stripes without fully appreciating what I had received. First Peter 2:24 (NKJV) declares that Jesus "bore our sins in His own body on the tree, that we, having died to sins, might live for righteousness—by whose stripes you were healed." Those healing stripes are the gaping wounds in Jesus's flesh left from the whipping Roman soldiers gave him before his crucifixion.

According to Roman tradition, soldiers scourged their victims with a short cluster of whips similar to what's known as a cat-o'-nine-tails. Each strand of leather had a sharp piece of bone or metal attached to the end of it. When struck across the body, it would rip off layers of skin in a strip several inches wide, causing excruciating pain and excessive bleeding. Jesus took numerous lashings with this type of whip across his torso and legs. After the Romans had mocked him and crowned him with a wreath of thorns, he had to carry his cross until he collapsed under its weight, before eventually being crucified. Though he was God in the flesh, we should never minimize the human suffering Jesus endured on our behalf.

In 1991, at the beginning of my career with the Los Angeles Dodgers, I received Jesus as my Savior by trusting in his sinless and sacrificial death, burial, and resurrection for the forgiveness of my sins and the promise of eternal life in heaven. Unfortunately, it took nearly fifteen years before I experienced Jesus's spiritual and emotional healing. That's when I came to truly know him as described in John 6:35, where Jesus says, "I am the bread of life; whoever comes to me shall not hunger, and whoever believes in me shall never thirst."

You see, I first received Jesus's free gift of salvation on my terms, not his. For years I related to Jesus like he was my copilot, but I never relinquished control of my flight plan. Jesus was my consultant, yet I maintained veto power on all decisions, or so I thought. Jesus was my friend but not my king, master, lord, owner, or boss. Instead of surrendering control of my life to

Christ, who promised me his abundant life in return, I foolishly remained a slave to my own passions, lusts, and desires. I thought I was in control, but my sinful desires controlled me. Since I was unwilling to let go of my old life, I couldn't realize God's best for my new life in Christ. My prayers for bailouts, exemptions, and favors from my heavenly Father only cheapened his invaluable grace. James 4:3–5 describes my condition exactly: "You ask and do not receive, because you ask wrongly, to spend it on your passions. You adulterous people! Do you not know that friendship with the world is enmity with God? Therefore whoever wishes to be a friend of the world makes himself an enemy of God. Or do you suppose it is to no purpose that the Scripture says, 'He yearns jealously over the spirit that he has made to dwell in us'?"

I am extremely thankful that God jealously loves us when we are unlovable. God's Word tells us to love our enemies because he did just that for you and me. Throughout my professional baseball career, I was a "friend of the world," doing worldly things, sowing to the desires of my flesh by living promiscuously and doing whatever made me feel good. That type of selfish, riotous living made me "an enemy of God" according to the Scriptures. But when I received God's gift of salvation in Jesus Christ, I was adopted into the family of God as a son of the One True King. What I didn't understand at the time was that to truly experience the abundant life Jesus promised, I had to get off the throne of my life so Christ could

For too long I thought I knew the way, but it was a lie that nearly killed me.

assume his rightful position. I had to relinquish control so that Jesus's power and authority might increase in my life. It would be many years and multiple wrong turns, dead ends, and detours along my faith journey before I understood Jesus's teaching in John 14:6: "I am the way, and the truth, and the life. No one comes to the Father except through me." For too long I thought I knew the way, but it was a lie that nearly killed me.

ERASING GOD OUT

King Solomon, the wisest man in biblical history, had all the riches, wisdom, and women he could enjoy, and by his own admission, he struck out at finding fulfillment. According to my count, in the first three chapters of Ecclesiastes, King Solomon uses "I" forty-six times. And yet, he sums up his life as "vanity" or futilely chasing the wind.

I used to be ego driven too. I'll define that attitude with an acronym: erase God out (EGO). My self-consumed perspective left no room for God in my life. I was commander-in-chief of my existence. But God is no one's vice president. He will not reside where he does not preside. He can't be a resident where he is not president. Philippians 2:9–11 states it well: "God has highly exalted him [Jesus] and bestowed on him the name that is above every name, so that at the name of Jesus every knee should bow, in heaven and on earth and under the earth, and every tongue confess that Jesus Christ is Lord, to the glory of God the Father."

Before and after retiring from baseball in 1999, I went through seasons of self-destruction driven by drug addiction and a narcissistic attitude. Because God is patient, he allowed me to reap the destruction I sowed. To be clear, God did not turn his back on me in my seasons of rebellion. But my sinful lifestyle distanced me from my Savior. I was the one who moved, not him.

God taught me this lesson in how my wife, Tracy, responded to me during our season of dating before we were married. When I first met Tracy, she was falling deeper and deeper in love with Jesus. She passionately pursued knowing him and the power of his resurrection in her life. God had replaced her appetite for drugs with a hunger and thirst for his Word. She glowed with the glory of Christ in her life and exhibited a joy and contentment that had always eluded me.

God is no one's vice president. He will not reside where he does not preside.

I, on the other hand, was trying to remain both a friend of the world and a follower of Jesus—a recipe for disaster. Yet Tracy was always so loving, forgiving, and gracious to me—firm but compassionate at the same time. She made it clear that she had no intention of going back to her old way of living and that I needed to choose my way or God's way; I couldn't have it both ways. That meant she wasn't going to compromise her relationship with Jesus by pursuing a dating relationship with me if I wasn't sold out to Jesus as well.

God used Tracy's singular desire for holiness to show me how God responds to sin. Just like Tracy, God was also patient and longsuffering during my seasons of rebellion. God never rejected me or gave up on me. But just as Tracy refused to allow our relationship to become more serious so long as I held on to my sinful lifestyle and habits, God will not dwell where sin resides. God was showing me through Tracy that holiness and sinfulness can't coexist.

Even more than Tracy's outer beauty, I was attracted to her inner beauty. Her life exhibited what the Bible calls in Galatians 5 the fruits of the Spirit: love, joy, peace, patience, kindness, goodness, faithfulness, gentleness, and self-control. After we were married, I still longed to have a relationship with God like Tracy did. When I prayerfully asked God why Tracy could hear from him but I couldn't, God told me, "Because she spends time with me." Then God spoke in his still, small voice and said, "If you want what Tracy has, then you are going to have to do what she does by spending time daily reading and meditating on my Word—the Holy Bible."

A NEW IDENTITY

Jesus reminds us in Matthew 6:24, "No one can serve two masters, for either he will hate the one and love the other, or he will be devoted to the one and despise the other. You cannot serve God and money." My wealth and fame were intoxicants that ruled my life for nearly twenty-five years. When I finally became sick and tired of being sick and tired, I cried out to God in repentance. Much like the prodigal son in the Gospel of Luke who, after literally wallowing with pigs, humbly returned to his welcoming father, I too immediately sensed God's comforting presence when I cried out to him. And this time I was ready to submit to Jesus as Lord. The implications of Jesus's lordship, or authority, over my life increasingly challenged me to take off the uniform of pride, or "put off the old self," and redefine my identity in Christ, like Paul writes about in Colossians 3: 5–10:

> Put to death therefore what is earthly in you: sexual immorality, impurity, passion, evil desire, and covetousness, which is idolatry. On account of these the wrath of God is coming. In these you too once walked, when you were living in them. But now you must put them all away: anger, wrath, malice, slander, and obscene talk from your mouth. Do not lie to one another, seeing that you have put off the old self with its practices and have put on the new self, which is being renewed in knowledge after the image of its creator.

When I started putting to death my old life, the true meaning and purpose of my new life came into focus. My behavior changed dramatically.

The nouns in my vocabulary also changed. In elementary school grammar, you learn that a noun is a person, place, or thing. Part of redefining my identity involved changing with whom and what I identified. That meant I could no longer hang out with the same people I partied with or dated. I couldn't go to the same places where those people congregated. I couldn't do the same things or watch the same entertainment as they did. The adjectives I used in my speech also changed. No longer did I employ those four-letter words and vulgar expressions to describe my thoughts and ideas.

Jesus Christ's invitation to follow him in Luke 9:23–24 includes a radical claim on my life and yours. He presents a conditional promise that offers a guaranteed return on investment like nothing I've ever heard of from any financial planner or investment portfolio manager. "If anyone would come after me, let him deny himself and take up his cross daily and follow me. For whoever would save his life will lose it, but whoever loses his life for my sake will save it."

Lose your life to save it? Save your life and lose it? On the surface, these propositions seem backward, right? But the realities are quite profound. Jesus isn't saying to think less of yourself but instead to think of yourself less. I had very little experience denying myself anything throughout much of my adult life. Me, myself, and I were the only quorum necessary to make a decision. Yet Jesus's command to take up my cross and follow him means I have to sacrifice anything that competes with his rightful position on the throne of my life. Denying myself means decisions have to be less about me and more of Christ in me—less of my ambitions and more of his priorities dictating my choices.

Jesus gives us a profound illustration of what losing your life to save it means in John 12:24–26: "Truly, truly, I say to you, unless a grain of wheat falls into the earth and dies, it remains alone; but if it dies, it bears much fruit. Whoever loves his life loses it, and whoever hates his life in this world will keep it for eternal life. If anyone serves me, he must follow me; and where I am, there will my servant be also. If anyone serves me, the Father will honor him."

Jesus is the master of bringing new life out of death. He did it on the cross, and he can do it again when you sacrifice your way of living for the life he wants to live through you. When we die to ourselves, Jesus promises to produce the fruits of the Spirit listed in Galatians 5:22–23: "love, joy, peace, patience, kindness, goodness, faithfulness, gentleness, self-control." That's exactly what I desire to see and experience more of in my life. How about you? I've come to realize that for that promise from God's Word to be a reality in my life, there has to be less of me and more of Christ in me.

Jesus is the master of bringing new life out of death.

TAKING CUES

Before stepping into the batter's box, I looked at my third base coach for his hand signals to either swing for the fences, take a pitch, lay down a sacrifice bunt, or hit the ball to the opposite field. Similarly, now I try to take my cues from Scripture and base my decisions on one question: "What would Jesus do?" Because of my identity in Christ, he is not just my friend or life coach; he is king over my life. I live to serve Jesus. Galatians 2:20

is my mission statement: "I have been crucified with Christ. It is no longer I who live, but Christ lives in me. And the life I now live in the flesh I live by faith in the Son of God, who loved me and gave himself for me." Now when I autograph a baseball card or some other memorabilia from my playing days, I tell fans and admirers I'm not the same person I was then. My heavenly Father created me for his glory and not my own, so I no longer crave the acceptance and validation of others. Knowing that God created me for his exclusive purposes validates my life more than any honor or accolade I achieved as a baseball player.

In Ephesians 2:10, the apostle Paul reminds Christ followers what it means to know Jesus as Savior and Lord: "We are his workmanship, created in Christ Jesus for good works, which God prepared beforehand, that we should walk in them."

I will be the first to admit that God gifted me with physical attributes and skills to excel in the sport of baseball. While most major leaguers have been hitting a baseball off a tee since age four or five, I didn't start playing until I was thirteen. Just five years into playing competitive baseball, I was the number one ranked player in the world in the amateur baseball draft. With less than three years in the minor leagues, I debuted with the New York Mets, where I was later named Rookie of the Year. I didn't take the most conventional route to baseball stardom, to say the least. Let's just say that being a six-foot, six-inch left-handed hitter with catlike reflexes and a silky-smooth swing presented certain challenges to opposing pitchers. It's not that I didn't have to work hard to be successful; the game of baseball requires too much skill to get by on just athleticism. But I had a knack for seeing the spinning, stitched cowhide-covered cork come out of the pitcher's hand. And I could sync the timing of my right leg lift and swing so that the sweet spot of the bat connected with the baseball at just the right time. My effortless-looking swing seemed to imply that I was born to play the game.

But my purpose was more than hitting home runs and winning World Series championships; God made me for an eternal purpose. Baseball brought me fame and fortune, but God created me to bring him glory. God's ultimate plan for my life was to take the mess I had made and turn it into his message of grace and forgiveness. And now that I'm running the race God created me for, I am more fulfilled than I ever was playing baseball.

> **God's ultimate plan for my life was to take the mess I had made and turn it into his message of grace and forgiveness.**

I've discovered something. As I starve my natural appetite for self-promotion and self-preservation, I increasingly desire more of what God wants for me. Psalm 34:8 exclaims, "Oh, taste and see that the LORD is good! Blessed is the man who takes refuge in him!" And it's true. The more I am willing to trust and obey God, the more I experience his refuge of peace and blessing.

The same holds true for you. Since God created you for his glory, doesn't it make sense that you would find your ultimate fulfillment in God's plans and purposes? Like a well-disciplined batter refraining from swinging at a pitch outside the strike zone and instead locking and unloading on a more hittable pitch, when we deny our self-serving instincts, we open ourselves up to connecting with God's best for our lives. To complete the baseball analogy, when the largest area on the barrel of a baseball bat—known as the "sweet spot"—makes contact with a baseball at just the right time, the farther and faster the baseball is launched. Similarly, when you leverage your time, talents, and treasure for God's glory, your life and the lives of others are changed forever. Retired legendary Dodgers play-by-play broadcaster Vin Scully is famous for describing a home run ball's flight by saying "forget it" as it sailed over the fence. But when you pursue the purposes God created you for, there's nothing forgettable about it. The results are life-changing and the impact is eternal.

SACRIFICE

In the game of baseball, with fewer than two outs in an inning, a batter can drive in a runner from third base by hitting a long fly ball for an out. In theory, the batter sacrifices himself by intentionally making an out. If the runner begins his sprint toward home plate after the outfielder catches the ball and beats the throw to the catcher, then the run scores. This is called a sacrifice fly. To describe such a play as a sacrifice is a bit of a misnomer. Yes, an out is made, but the batter gets credited in the box score with an RBI. Likewise, when we sacrifice our agenda, plans, or desires for what God desires, we stand to gain infinitely more than we sacrifice. The Lord has taught me this biblical principle on many occasions.

For example, I was selected for season nine of the wildly popular NBC television series *The Celebrity Apprentice*. This was a great opportunity to raise awareness for a charity my wife, Tracy, and I supported to help children with autism. But by week three of the competition, I asked the show's host and executive producer, Donald Trump, to fire me. Behind the scenes of the reality television series was an environment flowing with alcohol, reminiscent of the life I had forsaken to follow Jesus. So to remain faithful in my Christian walk and flee temptation, I voluntarily withdrew from the show. God's Word had taught me in 1 Corinthians 10:13, "No temptation has overtaken you that is not common to man. God is faithful, and he will not let you be tempted beyond your ability, but with the temptation he will also provide the way of escape, that you may be able to endure it." My voluntary exit of *The Celebrity Apprentice* proved to be an opportunity to obey God's Word by fleeing temptation. And in the end, God honored my obedience by protecting me from succumbing to choices that had repeatedly caused me to trip and fall in the past. Plus, out of respect for my personal convictions, Donald Trump donated $25,000 to the charity for autistic children.

Two years later God told Tracy and me to close Strawberry Sports Grill, the thriving restaurant we owned in Queens, New York. Business was booming. Some investment partners were planning to expand our restaurant brand to other locations in neighboring boroughs across New York City. My recent induction into the New York Mets Hall of Fame had sparked a resurgence of positive notoriety for a restaurant with my name on it. Friends and business associates alike were banking that "if you build it, they will come." And the timing seemingly couldn't have been better for my personal finances. Like the plague of locusts that devoured Egypt's vegetation when Pharaoh disobeyed God's commands to free the Israelites from slavery, the costs of my drug addiction had pillaged my financial security and rendered me several million dollars in debt. But the growth of my restaurant business seemed to be ushering in a new season—ripe for reaping.

So why was God leading me to walk away from an opportunity to cash in on my revived celebrity status and restore my financial stability?

He wanted me to lay down my identity as a former professional baseball player so I could know him as Jehovah Jireh, which means "my provider." God was teaching me to trust more in him and less in myself. He wanted me to deny myself, take up my cross, and follow him. Only then could I experience his realities beyond imagination (RBIs).

Both instances represented crossroads in my faith. If the Bible was authoritative for my life, I had to choose between my identity in Christ and the pursuit of fortune and fame. Was I going to trust in material success—replicating the business model of my highly profitable restaurant with solid financial backing for market expansion? Or was I going to take a step of faith into the unknown and follow God's prompting to preach the gospel? When I looked to Scripture for the answer to my dilemma, Hebrews 11:1 was unequivocally clear then and now: "Faith is the assurance of things hoped for, the conviction of things not seen."

FAITH FULL

We place our faith in people and things every day. Every time I board a plane to travel as an itinerant evangelist, I hope the pilot and airplane mechanic who certified the aircraft ready for flight have brought their A-game. When you eat at a restaurant, you hope the kitchen crew uses the freshest ingredients and washed their hands thoroughly prior to prepping the meal. If I exercise faith in those situations, how much more should I have faith in the One who hung the sun, moon, and stars and owns all the cattle on a thousand hills?

In Hebrews 11:6, the Bible declares that without faith, it's impossible to please God. I'm thankful God gave me the faith, courage, and boldness to walk away from those temptations of worldly gain. I'm reminded that Jesus faced a similar temptation when he was hungry after fasting for forty days and forty nights. When tempted by Satan in the wilderness to turn stones to bread to satisfy his hunger pains, Jesus replied in Matthew 4:4, "It is written, 'Man shall not live by bread alone, but by every word that comes from the mouth of God.'" I have found that believing and obeying God's Word empowers me to overcome my fears and insecurities. Reading the Bible and memorizing Scripture builds my faith and gives me wisdom and courage to trust God more in every decision I make. At first when God called me to preach the good news, I responded as Moses did when God called him to lead the Israelites out of slavery to Pharaoh in Egypt. *You've got the wrong guy. I'm not a public speaker. I'm not qualified.* I tried to reason with God, but the Holy Spirit reminded me that God doesn't call the qualified; he qualifies the called. That's what Jesus did when he called the twelve disciples to follow him and become fishers of men. At least seven of the disciples were fishermen by trade, and another **God doesn't call** was a tax collector, not exactly theologians in **the qualified;** their own right. The more time I spent reading **he qualifies** the Bible, memorizing Scripture, and praying **the called.** through God's promises in his Word, passages like John 14:26 became a reality in my life: "The Helper, the Holy Spirit, whom the Father will send in my name, he will teach you all things and bring to your remembrance all that I have said to you."

I couldn't avoid God's tag on my life any longer. He had called me out. But not like an umpire who rung me up for looking at strike three. God had called me to go out like his disciples to be a fisher of men and women, boys and girls, for his kingdom and the sake of the gospel. He had spoken clearly to me through Scripture. The Holy Spirit's prompting also resonated throughout my being. Furthermore, God was also speaking through my wife, Tracy, who had been prayerfully sensing God's leading in the same direction for my life. I finally came to realize that God had been preparing me over a seven-year period of studying the Scriptures, praying, and meditating on his Word while learning how to daily surrender control of my life to his perfect plan. Before commissioning me to serve him as an evangelist, the Lord allowed me to learn experientially what the Psalmist David writes about in Psalm 40:1–5:

> I waited patiently for the LORD;
>> he inclined to me and heard my cry.
> He drew me up from the pit of destruction,
>> out of the miry bog,
> and set my feet upon a rock,
>> making my steps secure.
> He put a new song in my mouth,
>> a song of praise to our God.
> Many will see and fear,
>> and put their trust in the LORD.
>
> Blessed is the man who makes
>> the LORD his trust,
> who does not turn to the proud,
>> to those who go astray after a lie!
> You have multiplied, O LORD my God,
>> your wondrous deeds and your thoughts toward us;
>> none can compare with you!
> I will proclaim and tell of them,
>> yet they are more than can be told.

God rescued me from the hopeless pit of my drug addiction and firmly established me in the Word of God. For seven years, I immersed myself in prayer and reading and studying the Bible at church and home. I hid God's Word in my heart by memorizing Scripture and prayed his promises over my life, marriage, and family. As I did this, I fell deeper in love with Jesus. Now that my identity is in Christ alone, the psalmist's declaration in this passage is all I want to give my days to for the remaining seasons of my life. If God can transform my life, no one stands beyond his touch. The good news of the gospel is without question the best news ever!

Upon receiving God's grace through faith in Jesus Christ, your identity is redefined. Formerly an enemy of God, you now become Christ's ambassador of reconciliation. It's like you've switched teams. No longer are you part of the earthly visiting team opposing God. Now, having been adopted into God's family, you are a member of the eternal heavenly home team.

In my MLB career, changing teams always came with mixed emotions. I didn't want to leave the New York Mets. After all, they were the first team to believe in me and give me a chance to play in the big leagues when they chose me with the first pick in the 1980 amateur baseball draft. I experienced the firsts of many feats with the Mets. My first hit, first run, first home run, first All-Star selection, first division championship, pennant, and World Series championship. But years later, when my contract was up, the Los Angeles Dodgers came calling. This presented an opportunity to play for my hometown team. And as hard as it was to leave the Mets, there's no better feeling than being wanted by the team you grew up idolizing, especially when they're willing to pay you more to play for them. But all that pales in comparison to being chosen for God's team at a price infinitely higher than all the money in the world.

In 2 Corinthians 5:19–21, the apostle Paul describes the greatest team trade in human history: "In Christ God was reconciling the world to himself, not counting their trespasses against them, and entrusting to us the message of reconciliation. Therefore, we are ambassadors for Christ, God making his appeal through us. We implore you on behalf of Christ, be reconciled to God. For our sake he made him to be sin who knew no sin, so that in him we might become the righteousness of God."

It is unbelievably humbling to know God chose me for his team not because of my talent or skill but despite my imperfections, shortcomings, and sinful nature. In essence, God voided my no-trade clause and paid the astronomical buyout penalty on my lifetime contract with death—the wages for my sin, as the Bible says. Then upon my joining his team, God suited me up in his uniform of righteousness, equipping, empowering, and enabling me to do supernatural feats such as loving unconditionally, forgiving exponentially, and serving selflessly. And every day, I walk in victory, declaring that anyone and everyone can be made right with God through faith in Jesus's death, burial, and resurrection for the forgiveness of sin and promise of eternal life.

THINK ABOUT IT

1. What does it mean to be a "friend of the world"?
2. What does Jesus mean when he describes himself as "the way, and the truth, and the life"?
3. If you were to confess that "Jesus Christ is Lord," what differences would that make in your life?
4. You are God's "workmanship." He has created you for a purpose. How would you define that purpose?
5. To what degree is money a master of your life?
6. How might you "lose your life" for Jesus's sake? What sacrifices might he ask of you?
7. Reread 1 Corinthians 10:13. What does that verse promise about temptation? How could you remember that when you're being tempted?
8. What does it mean to be an ambassador for Christ?

3RD INNING

RENEW YOUR MIND

> Trust in the LORD with all your heart,
>   and do not lean on your own understanding.
> In all your ways acknowledge him,
>   and he will make straight your paths.

PROVERBS 3:5–6

In the sport of baseball, a player's mental approach to the game can largely determine success or failure. When competing against the most skilled and athletic players in the world, a competitive advantage often is achieved more by what's going on between the ears than between the lines on the field. As a major leaguer, I tried to approach each at bat or each play in the field as a new opportunity to succeed. That meant my previous at bat or last twenty at bats, for better or worse, should have no bearing on my focus and outlook for success in the moment at hand. Each at bat as well as the next play in the field should stand on its own as a moment of truth. I literally had to renew my mind from pitch to pitch. Otherwise, the disappointment, frustration, or elation from one pitch, catch, swing, or throw to the next could distract me from being my best during the next opportunity.

The ability to refocus my mind in the course of a game propelled me to deliver some big moments for my team. In the 1986 National League Championship Series between the New York Mets and Houston Astros, determining who would go to the World Series, my batting average was a paltry .227. In fact, I struck out twelve out of twenty-two at bats. After amassing twenty-seven home runs and ninety-three RBIs in leading the Mets to 108 victories during the regular season, I could have gotten discouraged about this playoff slump, but thinking about my past failures at the plate would only have distracted me in the present and further compromised my struggling swing. Instead, I embraced each at bat as the next opportunity for success. In game three of the series, I hit a three-run homer to tie the score in a game we eventually won. And in game five, I hit a 94-mile-per-hour fastball from Hall of Fame Pitcher Nolan Ryan over the right field fence in Shea Stadium to tie the game. That homer is the most special of my career because it came off Ryan, who pitched a record seven no-hitters during his epic career, which spanned four decades. We eventually won that game in extra innings. Then in game six, I hit a double in the sixteenth inning and scored the go-ahead run as the Mets won the pennant.

Statistically, we shouldn't have won that series. Astros pitchers held my beloved Mets to the lowest team batting average (.189) of any National League Pennant winner in history. But a renewed state of mind gave me and the Mets new life. In essence, the baseball fundamentals you learn in Little League, such as "always keep your eye on the ball" and "keep your head in the game," are lessons that serve you well all the way to the major leagues. But the biggest lesson is what I learned after all those strikeouts: "Don't dwell on past mistakes."

The apostle Paul teaches this in Philippians 3:13–14: "Brothers, I do not consider that I have made it my own. But one thing I do: forgetting what lies behind and straining forward to what lies ahead, I press on toward the goal for the prize of the upward call of God in Christ Jesus."

This is winning advice for baseball and life. Every game and every day can be a new opportunity to succeed, develop, and grow even in the midst of mistakes or failure. A 162-game Major League Baseball season can become a grind by mid- to late summer. Add spring training on the front end and the playoffs and World Series on the back end of a season, and I was lacing up the cleats for nearly nine months of the year. If my baseball coaches said it once, they said it a million times: "Don't dwell on the past. You can't get to the new if you're still holding on to the old. Yesterday will never win today's

You can't get to the new if you're still holding on to the old. Yesterday will never win today's game.

game. Focus on the challenge in front of you. You can't move forward looking backward." Hindsight, as they say, is twenty-twenty. And while we should learn from the past, time is too precious and fleeting to stay there. Should have, could have, and would have never accomplished much. The same is true for experiencing new life in Christ. Every day that God gives you and me air in our lungs to take our next breath and commands our heart to beat in rhythm is another day to experience his grace and mercy.

HUMAN WISDOM

In the game of life, a Christian can daily renew his or her mind in the precepts of God's Word, where we find the fundamentals for godly living in an ungodly world. The Bible warns us not to be enamored of human wisdom: "See to it that no one takes you captive by philosophy and empty deceit, according to human tradition, according to the elemental spirits of the world, and not according to Christ" (Colossians 2:8).

In today's world, where conventional wisdom tells you to chase your dreams, trust your instincts, follow your heart, pursue your truth, and do what makes you happy, why do we see a deadly opioid epidemic, burgeoning suicide rate, growing consumer debt crisis, and escalating gun violence? The answer is because the culture's way of thinking is guided by counterfeit truths, deceptive motives, and vain ambition. Human wisdom will inevitably leave you physically, emotionally, financially, intellectually, and more importantly, spiritually bankrupt.

Renewing your mind according to the Bible enables you to distinguish between human wisdom and heavenly wisdom. The Old Testament prophet Isaiah describes such godly wisdom in Isaiah 55:8–9:

> For my thoughts are not your thoughts,
>> neither are your ways my ways, declares the LORD.
> For as the heavens are higher than the earth,
>> so are my ways higher than your ways
>> and my thoughts than your thoughts.

How wise is your God? The psalmist declares that God knows your thoughts and what you are going to do or say before you do or say it. He has numbered your days from the first to the last. He has created you for good works that he prepared for you while you were in your mother's womb. How big is your God? Before the foundation of the world the Father, Son, and Holy Spirit were there as God spoke the world into creation, the book of Genesis declares. He tells the sun when to rise and set. He holds earth suspended in space at just the precise distance from the sun so that the planet doesn't ice over or burst into flames. The ocean tides advance and recede at God's command.

So who are you going to listen to?

The wisest man in Scripture warns of the vanity of human wisdom. In Ecclesiastes 2:14–17, King Solomon writes:

The wise person has his eyes in his head, but the fool walks in darkness. And yet I perceived that the same event happens to all of them. Then I said in my heart, "What happens to the fool will happen to me also. Why then have I been so very wise?" And I said in my heart that this also is vanity. For of the wise as of the fool there is no enduring remembrance, seeing that in the days to come all will have been long forgotten. How the wise dies just like the fool! So I hated life, because what is done under the sun was grievous to me, for all is vanity and a striving after wind.

In pride, we think we can outsmart, outmaneuver, outrun, even outlive the consequences of our transgressions. But no level of intelligence, wealth, power, or prestige can provide an escape for our appointed time to die. As the COVID-19 pandemic reminds us, death is no respecter of persons. We must each give an account to God for what we did with his love, grace, and wisdom.

And yet in modern times, "striving after the wind" has become its own commercialized industry. In a world of 24/7 broadcast news, incessant political commentary and debate, sports talk, infomercials, traffic and weather updates, streaming movies, and music on demand, human wisdom dominates our lives. Clearly there is no shortage of communication streams competing for our attention. Whether we're tethered to our wireless devices, posting and trolling social media accounts, gaming with friends, surfing the internet for knowledge about what's trending, self-diagnosing our latest malady, planning our next excursion, or researching investment strategies, the digital information age has unleashed an endless barrage of messages and confusing noise. First Corinthians 3:18–20 issues a sobering warning about the wisdom of this world: "Let no one deceive himself. If anyone among you thinks that he is wise in this age, let him become a fool that he may become wise. For the wisdom of this world is folly with God. For it is written, 'He catches the wise in their craftiness,' and again, 'The Lord knows the thoughts of the wise, that they are futile.'"

THE SOURCE

In the twenty-first century, with the most knowledge in human history at our fingertips, only one source still addresses the plight of humankind since the beginning of time and answers the age-old question: What is the meaning of life?

"All Scripture is breathed out by God and profitable for teaching, for reproof, for correction, and for training in righteousness, that the man of God may be complete, equipped for every good work" (2 Timothy 3:16–17).

These Bible verses teach us that God directed the human authors of the Bible. Divine inspiration distinguishes the Holy Bible as universally and timelessly authoritative, unlike any other work of literature in the world. Scripture records the history of civilization from creation to the birth, death, resurrection, and heavenly ascension of Jesus Christ and the spread of Christianity throughout Asia and the Middle East. God's Word is infinitely valuable for teaching what to believe and what not to believe and how to act and how not to act.

Yet biblical wisdom remains largely an untapped resource even among those who call themselves Christians. An American Bible Society and Barna Group 2019 "State of the Bible" phone and online survey of about two thousand people across all fifty states revealed that more than one-third of those surveyed (31 percent) never read the Bible—a 10 percent increase since 2011.[1] Some reported interacting with the Bible frequently and said it transformed their relationships and shaped their choices, but this group dropped from 9 percent in 2018 to 5 percent in 2019. Furthermore, a 2019 LifeWay Research online survey of 2,500 Protestant churchgoers revealed that only about one-third (32 percent) of regular church attendees say they read the Bible personally every day. About 12 percent admitted they rarely or never read the Bible. Obviously, too many people are looking to Google, Siri, and Alexa for answers instead of the Holy Bible.

Information overload leads many people to stress out and seek escape through drugs or entertainment or isolate themselves from the chaos around them. If you find yourself doing this, you don't have to be discouraged, disillusioned, or defeated. These emotions don't have to define you. They are merely the side effects of focusing on your circumstances instead of the One who is sovereign over your predicament. God is bigger than your situation. He said he will never leave you nor forsake you. And the primary ways God fulfills that promise is through his abiding presence in his Word and in the Holy Spirit. The Bible is where we are reminded and reassured of God's faithfulness and empowered by his promises.

Jesus says in John 15:5, "I am the vine; you are the branches. Whoever abides in me and I in him, he it is that bears much fruit, for apart from me you can do nothing." Jesus teaches us in this passage that before you or I can do anything of eternal value in his name or experience his everlasting peace, we must

Too many people are looking to Google, Siri, and Alexa for answers instead of the Holy Bible.

first have our being or identity in him. To abide in Christ is to accept his will and his ways as your own. When you abide in Christ, you find your passion and purpose in his passion and purpose. You see people as Jesus sees people. You love others as Jesus loves them. You serve as Jesus served. You perceive and interpret the world around you from Jesus's perspective. And you are able to do this by having the mind of Christ, by thinking as Jesus thinks.

MENTAL RENEWAL

The Bible is full of instruction on the spiritual discipline of renewing your mind. For starters, the apostle Paul states clearly and succinctly in Romans 12:1–2, "I appeal to you therefore, brothers, by the mercies of God, to present your bodies as a living sacrifice, holy and acceptable to God, which is your spiritual worship. Do not be conformed to this world, but be transformed by the renewal of your mind, that by testing you may discern what is the will of God, what is good and acceptable and perfect."

As a professional athlete, I discovered that the more I took care of my body off the field, the more it took care of me on the field. Eating healthy, getting plenty of rest, and working out to keep my abs and legs strong were key to success in baseball.

Similarly, the apostle Paul taught that a Christ follower should avoid engaging in anything that might contradict Jesus's character. Holy means separate, sacred, or set apart. Just like my baseball uniform distinguished me and my teammates from everyone else in the stadium, a Christian's conduct should differentiate himself or herself from the world's acceptable standards of behavior. In the same way that the team uniform is the dress code between the lines on game day, Christ followers represent Jesus every day, for better or worse, in everything we do and say and everywhere we go. And just like I'm no less married with or without my wedding band on my left ring finger, a Christian is to live the Christian walk each day, not exclusively at church on Sunday. God calls Christians to be living sacrifices by exemplifying Christ wherever, whenever, and in whatever situations comes their way.

My relationship with Jesus is not something I can stow away only to be used when I need it, like my baseball helmet and bat in the dugout cubby. When the apostle Paul tells us to present our bodies as a living sacrifice, holy and acceptable to God, he is reminding Christians that our bodies are the temple of the Holy

Spirit. Consequently, before choosing to participate or become involved in any type of activity, we would do well to ask ourselves, "Would God be glorified by such actions?"

Discovering God's will for your life doesn't have to be some mysterious exploration of trial and error. God isn't standing on the pitcher's mound trying to make you swing and miss at his curveball or slider. Worldly wisdom teaches that you can "find yourself" by experimenting with various curiosities, relationships, philosophies, or religions. Along life's winding journey, your "true self" will morph out of the accumulation of your experiences, the good, the bad, and the ugly, philosophers opine. Don't buy this mumbo jumbo. To do so would be to conform to the world's way of thinking. The randomization of such fateful choices was never God's plan for our lives. The Bible clearly tells us that by renewing our minds with the Word of God, we can know what God's good, acceptable, and perfect plan is for our individual lives. In this powerfully challenging passage, Paul encourages Christians not to mirror the culture's stinking thinking or me-first mentality. Don't be deceived and seduced by an "American Dream" obsessed with prominence, power, and possessions. Instead of allowing the culture to squeeze you into its mold by conforming you to its worldly, humanistic mindset, Christ followers are called to break the mold and pursue God's will above their own. Proverbs 19:21 provides godly wisdom we would do well to heed: "Many are the plans in the mind of a man, but it is the purpose of the LORD that will stand."

When you renew your mind according to biblical principles,

your way of thinking reflects the mind of Christ as described in Hebrews 12:2: "Looking to Jesus, the founder and perfecter of our faith, who for the joy that was set before him endured the cross, despising the shame, and is seated at the right hand of the throne of God." Jesus thought of others more than himself. Putting sinners' needs before his own, he suffered and died on a cross so we could live victoriously on earth and forever with him in heaven.

Jesus fulfilled God's will on earth. Likewise, Christ followers are called to be living sacrifices by following Jesus's example. He taught that if someone strikes you on the cheek, you should not strike back but turn the other cheek. He said that those who store up for themselves treasures on earth do so in vain. Whoever wants to be great, Jesus said, must be a servant like him. Yes, following Christ is often countercultural, anti-instinctive, and defies popular opinion or conventional wisdom, but this is the mind of Christ. This is his way.

MORE THAN FANS

One of my favorite Bible passages in all of Scripture is Proverbs 3:5–6:

> Trust in the LORD with all your heart,
>   and do not lean on your own understanding.
> In all your ways acknowledge him,
>   and he will make straight your paths.

To trust in the Lord with all your heart means to be "all in" with Jesus. Admittedly, this is easier said than done. "All in with Jesus" looks great on a T-shirt or bumper sticker. But the practical application of trusting in the Lord with all your heart will have radical implications on how you live your life.

Your heart is the epicenter for your dreams, ambitions, goals, desires, passions, and emotions—sort of your personal home plate. Just imagine what it might look like to surrender your life's motivation, quest for fulfillment, and measure of success to the Lord. This is what separates fans from followers when it comes to trusting the Lord with all your heart and not leaning on what you think you know.

When I played for the New York Mets, Los Angeles Dodgers, San Francisco Giants, and New York Yankees, my fan base directly correlated with the uniform I wore. Fans of those teams rooted for me as a team member. I will never forget, however, the game when I hit a home run in Shea Stadium, not with the home team Mets but with the crosstown rival Yankees.

At the time, I held the record for hitting the most home runs in Shea Stadium. I had played there for eight seasons, hitting 126 dingers, and every time the Big Apple symbol would mechanically rise up behind the outfield wall in celebration of the hometown hero as the Mets fans went wild. But my 127th home run in that park came as a visitor wearing the Yankee pinstripes.

As I rounded the bases, I saw the iconic Big Apple beginning its ascent just as it did every time a Met player homered. I guess the operator forgot I was hitting bombs for the Yankees that day.

About the time the Mets logo came into view, someone must have realized the mistake, and the Big Apple retreated as quickly as it had risen. But Mets fans did not stop standing and clapping until I stepped on the top step of the visitors' dugout and waved to the adoring crowd. A player from the visiting team rarely receives a standing ovation from the hometown crowd. Most of those in attendance at Shea Stadium weren't Yankee fans by any stretch of the imagination. But they were my fans, and I appreciated that.

Fans play a huge role in sports. They encourage and inspire athletes to perform their best and to never give up. They celebrate in the victories and console in the losses. But fans aren't there during the predawn runs, weight-lifting workouts, closed practice sessions, or injury rehab stints. And fans don't hit the home runs, make the plays, score the runs, or make the outs. In sports, to be all in means you are in the game. It's no different when it comes to trusting in the Lord with all your heart.

Jesus didn't leave his perfect heaven and come to earth to recruit fans. The fans who shouted "Hosanna!" and waved palm branches as Jesus rode into Jerusalem on a donkey were the same crowd that shouted "Crucify him!" just a few days later. When Jesus recruited his disciples, his call was clear—stop what you're doing and follow me. Act like me. Talk like me. Do what I do. Jesus called his disciples to be "fishers of men." As the disciples walked and talked with Jesus, he taught them what it means to trust in the Lord with all your heart. At first they debated among themselves who would be the greatest in Jesus's kingdom. Jesus told them that to be the greatest would require they drink from the same cup of suffering that he would drink, to which they naively and readily agreed.

So how did that work out for Jesus's disciples, you might ask. Ancient church traditions give us accounts of what happened after the book of Acts. Philip was strapped to a pillar and stoned to death. Matthew was staked to the ground with spikes and beheaded. Jude was pummeled to death with sticks and clubs. Simon the Zealot was tortured and crucified. John, son of Zebedee, was tortured and exiled to the island of Patmos. James, brother of John, was beheaded. The other James was pushed off the top of a building, then his broken body was beaten to death. Andrew hung on a cross for three days before dying. Bartholomew was beaten, skinned alive, and crucified before being beheaded. Thomas was tossed into a fiery furnace, then speared with a javelin. And Peter was crucified upside down. All of Jesus's beloved disciples except John died a martyr's death because they trusted in the risen Lord with all their heart. Had the disciples instead depended on their own understanding, they would have cowardly denied that Jesus had risen from the grave. Yet the disciples refused to cave in, despite violent attempts to snuff out the spread of Christianity.

You might think it unfair that the disciples' faithful obedience cost them their lives. If that's what it looks like when God makes your path straight, then no thanks, you might say. Those responses would be typical for someone leaning on their own understanding. But the disciples understood that to live is Christ and to die is gain. And in the crucial moment, they realized their deaths were a portal to heaven.

Today, being a Christ follower will likely not demand of you a martyr's death, but the cost is far greater than any club suite ticket price. Bottom line: Christianity is not a spectator sport. True worship is not cheering for Jesus; it's loving and serving him with all your heart, soul, mind, and strength. The culture's measure of success is about being served, but Jesus's measure of success is serving others. The Bible teaches us that Jesus came to the world not to be served but to serve and give his life as a ransom for many. Are you a Jesus fan or a Jesus follower? Evaluate your relationship with Jesus on his terms and not your own. Answer the question honestly and not wishfully. Then, if necessary, renew your mind according to God's Word and recommit your life to follow in faithful obedience. And then watch how God shows up and shows off in your life. When you commit to the process of renewing your mind through Scripture, you will increasingly desire what God desires. Your life will exemplify Jesus in word and deed. In other words, by God's grace you will talk the talk and walk the walk when God's Word is the instruction manual for your life.

True worship is not cheering for Jesus; it's loving and serving him with all your heart.

GOD'S CLAIM ON YOUR LIFE

In the previous chapters, we've unpacked some of God's spiritual RBIs—realities beyond imagination—for the abundant life Jesus promises. If you have received God's grace through faith in Jesus Christ, you have a new identity.

And with your new identity in Christ, through the power of the Holy Spirit that lives in you, you can renew your mind to think like Christ and emulate him. Paul's reminder to the Christians in Corinth compels Christ followers today to glorify God with every ounce of their being: "Do you not know that your body is a temple of the Holy Spirit within you, whom you have from God? You are not your own, for you were bought with a price. So glorify God in your body" (1 Corinthians 6:19–20).

It was not only my sinful practices that led to my fall but also my refusal to embrace God's ownership of my life. At some point, we must take responsibility for our actions. Even though the pain of the past is valid, it is never an excuse to continue in sin—addictions, ungodly desires, lust, other bad behaviors, or destructive living—which causes pain to ourselves and others. It's never okay to excuse away our rebellion against a holy and righteous God.

God's claim on your life began before you were born. In Psalm 139:13–16 we read:

> You formed my inward parts;
>> you knitted me together in my mother's womb.
> I praise you, for I am fearfully and wonderfully made.
> Wonderful are your works;
>> my soul knows it very well.
> My frame was not hidden from you,

> when I was being made in secret,
>
>   intricately woven in the depths of the earth.
>
> Your eyes saw my unformed substance;
>
> in your book were written, every one of them,
>
>   the days that were formed for me,
>
>   when as yet there was none of them.

The Bible, God's love letter to humanity, describes how he intricately fashioned you in your mother's womb. At no stage of your growth and development inside your mother's uterus are you any less human or less than a masterpiece of the Creator's design. His eyes are on you from the moment of your conception until your last breath, and he purposed every day in between according to his plans. You are not an accident or a mistake. God assigned your gender when he fearfully and wonderfully made you. He created you in his image with a soul and spirit that can be satisfied only in a thriving relationship with him. Acknowledging those realities, then, doesn't it make sense to embrace the identity and mindset the Bible prescribes—that you exist to bring God glory by fulfilling his purposes? Any other conclusion would be like me trying to hit a ninety-five-mile-per-hour fastball without swinging a bat—ludicrously insane.

Just like I wouldn't step into the batter's box without my bat, God doesn't expect us to face our tests and challenges without his guidance. Psalm 139 declares further that God knows you better than you know yourself. The psalmist says the Lord is "acquainted with all my ways." There's nowhere we can go to flee from God's presence. Camp out with that reality for a while. That means God is with us in every situation, good or bad. With every temptation, God is there as well. Even when we fall into sin, God is still there. No matter the stranglehold sin has on your life, its grip is not stronger than God's grip on you. He never abandons us in our moments of weakness. Because he is always there, he stands ready to strengthen us, lift us up, and walk with us through the fiery trials and deep waters.

God longs to heal the brokenhearted. Claim the promise from God's Word that when you are weak, he is your strength.

As I travel the country, everywhere I preach, men share with me their struggles with pornography. Their shame, guilt, despair, and isolation are overwhelming. The statistics tracking pornography's seduction of our culture are heartbreaking. Covenant Eyes, a ministry that offers internet filtering services and accountability measures to block pornographic consumption online, reports that 64 percent of Christian men and 15 percent of Christian women surveyed said they view pornography at least once a month. The ministry also reports that, on average, every second $3,075.64 is being spent on internet porn, and 28,258 users are watching it. And in 56 percent of divorce cases, one party reports having "an obsessive interest in pornographic websites."[2] If you are enslaved to pornography, you're not alone. Cry out to God in repentance, install internet filtering technology to block pornography online, and invite your spouse or a Christian of the same sex to help hold you accountable. Again, claim God's promise early and often that he will provide a way of escape from temptation. And the next time you feel tempted by the likes of pornography or any other questionable thought, desire, or activity, ask yourself if its pursuit or follow-through would exemplify Philippians 4:8: "Whatever is true, whatever is honorable, whatever is just, whatever is pure, whatever is lovely, whatever is commendable, if there is any excellence, if there is anything worthy of praise, think about these things."

REPROGRAMMING

Is your mind fully engaged in the game of life? Are you playing by God's rules? Do you daily reprogram your sin-natured default drive with the Word of God? Are you checking your heart and emotions according to Scripture? Are your thoughts and motives filtered through the Word of God? Do you look in the mirror of God's Word to see your true self? Are you pursuing God's will for your life and not your own? Hebrews 4:12–13 declares the power and authority the Word of God has over our lives: "The word of God is living and active, sharper than any two-edged sword, piercing to the division of soul and of spirit, of joints and of marrow, and discerning the thoughts and intentions of the heart. And no creature is hidden from his sight, but all are naked and exposed to the eyes of Him to whom we must give account."

If our Creator is going to judge us according to the Word of God, wouldn't it behoove us to saturate our lives in Scripture and meditate on God's Word so that we can discern his will for our lives? It's been said that you can fool most people some of the time and some people most of the time, but you can't fool God any of the time. Don't let the Enemy, Satan, deceive you into rationalizing your sin or justifying wrong motives. Comparing yourself to others only feeds your pride and incites jealousy, lust, and covetousness. Only the living Word of God can cut with precision like a surgeon's knife and expose sin that hides undetected like a deadly cancer.

Your willingness to trust and obey God speaks volumes about what you truly believe about him. The saying "actions speak louder than words" is more than a cliché. It's profoundly true. In Jeremiah chapter 17, the Lord rebuked the Israelites for trusting in their own sufficiency and following the inclinations of their heart, which led to idolatry. But for those who trusted and obeyed God, blessings followed.

> "Blessed is the man who trusts in the Lord,
>   whose trust is the Lord.
> He is like a tree planted by water,
>   that sends out its roots by the stream,
> and does not fear when heat comes,
>   for its leaves remain green,
> and is not anxious in the year of drought,
>   for it does not cease to bear fruit."
>
> The heart is deceitful above all things,
>   and desperately sick;

who can understand it?
"I the Lord search the heart
and test the mind,
to give every man according to his ways,
according to the fruit of his deeds."

As I write this book, our world is experiencing a global pandemic of the coronavirus, or COVID-19, the likes of which has not been experienced since the Spanish flu of 1918. To control the spread of this highly contagious and deadly virus, the world came to a screeching halt with mandatory closing of schools, churches, sporting events, concerts, and businesses. Shelter-in-place orders, self-quarantine protocols, and social distancing turned the world into a lonely place. Panic buying left grocery store shelves barren of toilet paper, eggs, flour, meats, and disinfecting wipes. Elective surgical procedures had to be postponed. Automobile manufacturers started making ventilators. Whiskey distilleries turned their alcohol into hand sanitizer. The stock market plummeted as millions lost their jobs.

In crises like this, we see the effect of having a renewed mind. Here we discover where our trust really is. Those who trust in the Lord during these uncertain times are unmistakable. Instinctive fears don't linger in their lives. Instead of worrying about their own future, those who trust in the Lord invest in the future of others by serving and showing them the love of Christ.

THINK ABOUT IT

1. How can you acknowledge God "in all your ways"?
2. What does it mean to "present your body as a living sacrifice" to God?
3. In what ways do you need to "renew your mind"?
4. If you're dealing with a porn addiction, whom could you ask to hold you accountable?
5. If your body is "the temple of the Holy Spirit," how should you treat it?
6. How can you know what God wants for your life?
7. How could you become more than just a fan of Jesus?

REVEAL YOUR SCARS

We know that for those who love God all
things work together for good, for those
who are called according to his purpose.

ROMANS 8:28

Americans spent more than $16.5 billion on cosmetic plastic surgery and minimally invasive procedures in 2018—a four-percent increase from the previous year—according to the American Society of Plastic Surgeons.[1] Our culture seems obsessed with outward appearances. Photoshopped images from magazine covers to social media posts propagate our society's quest for physical perfection. And while many don't go under the knife or needle for physical enhancement, most of us have perfected our "I'm okay" facade to mask our inner brokenness.

I can definitely relate. I did this for most of my life. As a baseball star, I was the picture of success—literally!—with seven appearances on the cover of *Sports Illustrated*. But on the inside, I was tormented by insecurity and confusion over my father's physical and emotional abuse. His sporadic absence throughout my childhood left me feeling rejected and confused. I think, however, if we're honest with ourselves, everyone grapples with their own fears and insecurities at some point in their lives. Call it the by-product of imperfect human beings being raised by imperfect human beings while coexisting with other imperfect human beings in an imperfect world.

The amazing news is that despite our imperfections, we have a perfect, sinless Savior who took on our sinful imperfections when he was nailed to a cross some two thousand years ago. The Old Testament prophet Isaiah foretold in Isaiah 53:3–6 of the Suffering Servant by whose wounds we can be healed:

> He was despised and rejected by men,
> > a man of sorrows and acquainted with grief;
> and as one from whom men hide their faces,
> > he was despised, and we esteemed him not.
>
> Surely he has borne our griefs
> > and carried our sorrows;
> yet we esteemed him stricken,
> > smitten by God, and afflicted.
> But he was pierced for our transgressions;
> > he was crushed for our iniquities;

upon him was the chastisement that brought us peace,

and with his wounds we are healed.

All we like sheep have gone astray;

we have turned—every one—to his own way;

and the LORD has laid on him

the iniquity of us all.

Ponder the reality of this fulfilled prophecy. Jesus Christ, the perfect, sinless Son of God, was scorned, rejected, and publicly humiliated by being nailed naked and bloodied to a cross. Even though he was innocent, Jesus, who was God in the flesh, subjected himself to his subjects. In other words, the creator of the universe voluntarily submitted his glorious perfection, majesty, power, and authority to the hands of those he had created. Don't miss this. Jesus didn't surrender his deity, and he wasn't a martyr. Martyrs willingly sacrifice their lives for causes bigger than themselves by taking stands that seal their fate. But martyrs can't control when and how they die. At any moment, Jesus could have commanded legions of angels to free him from the cross and spare him the violent, dehumanizing torture of crucifixion. When Christ hung on the cross between two thieves, he did not submit to the will of the Roman government—but to the will of his Father in heaven. And he did this because of his unfathomable love for you and me.

First Peter 2:24 explains, "He himself bore our sins in his body on the tree, that we might die to sin and live to righteousness. By his wounds you have been healed." Jesus willingly revealed his wounds on an old rugged cross atop Golgotha's hill so you and I could be healed of ours.

SCARS AND STORIES

Often when a wound heals, a scar is left in its place. When Jesus appeared to his disciples after his resurrection from the tomb, he convinced Thomas it was really him by showing his nail-scarred wrists and pierced side. John 20:26–28 provides the following account: "Eight days later, his disciples were inside again, and Thomas was with them. Although the doors were locked, Jesus came and stood among them and said, 'Peace be with you.' Then he said to Thomas, 'Put your finger here, and see my hands; and put out your hand, and place it in my side. Do not disbelieve, but believe.' Thomas answered him, 'My Lord and my God!'"

You see, our scars tell a story. And I'm convinced God is glorified when we share the stories about our physical and emotional scars as evidence of the wounds he's healed in our lives and the strength he's given us to endure and overcome.

When I think about my scars from two cancer surgeries, I'm reminded of God's mercy and faithfulness. In 1998 I played 101 games with the New York Yankees—the first year I had played more than 100 games since my last All-Star season with the Los Angeles Dodgers in 1991. It was great to be playing on a regular basis again.

Still, I did not feel well most of the season and took a lot of antacid medication every day just to get by. Toward the end of the season, I was passing blood and noticeably losing weight, so I had to admit something was seriously wrong. While my teammates got into the playoffs and swept the World Series, I went to the hospital.

Surgeons removed a cancerous tumor from my colon. Little did I know at the time how God was protecting me even as I recklessly disregarded my symptoms throughout much of the baseball season. The doctors said my abdominal muscles had been holding the tumor in place whenever I swung a bat or slid into a base. If not for those muscles, it could have burst and spread the cancer throughout my body. But God's plan for my life wasn't going to be thwarted even by cancer. I returned to the Yankees for the 1999 World Series championship season—my seventeenth year in the big leagues—before retiring from the game I had played since I was 13 years old.

The following year, cancer came back with a vengeance. This time the tumor was growing under my left kidney. But my outlook on life with the second cancer diagnosis was much different from the first. I was out of Major League Baseball for the first time in my adult life and ready to check out of life altogether. My drug use and partying lifestyle had again spiraled out of control. I was basically a junkie looking for my next fix before the cancer curveball benched me from the partying game. I told my doctors I didn't want to go through another surgery. I had nothing to live for and, frankly, hoped the malignancy would take my life sooner rather than later. But I hesitantly agreed to the surgery.

As the anesthesia slowly escorted me into a field of dreams, I hoped never to wake up again. When I reluctantly awoke to my postsurgery future, doctors informed me they had to remove my healthy left kidney to successfully extract the cancerous tumor beneath. The prognosis for a complete recovery from cancer's second assault on my body looked promising. But my outlook on the future seemed hopeless. Now when I think about my surgical scar, it reminds me how God used my second bout with cancer to save me from the throes of a drug addiction relapse that would surely have killed me. Before my hospitalization for the second cancer surgery, crack cocaine had become my best friend. But for the grace of God, I should never have survived drug binges that lasted for days. God could have easily turned me over to my reprobate mind, yet he refused to give up on me.

God had a plan to use my life to display his rescuing, redeeming, and restoring power. What the Enemy, Satan, had meant for evil in my life, God has used for his glory and my good. Romans 8:28 is one my life verses: "We know that for those who love God all things work together for good, for those who are called according to his purpose." The implication of this promise from God's Word is a game changer. In the game of baseball, when the umpire yells, "Strike three," the batter is rendered useless—that opportunity is lost. But in life, God has a three-letter word that can turn a strikeout into balling out for his glory. It's spelled A-L-L.

When Romans 8:28 says "all things," it clearly means that God can take any situation—yes, that includes our failures, mistakes, pain, and suffering—and bring good out of it. All means all. But here's the catch—you have to be willing to lay down your pride and surrender to God your brokenness, weakness, fear, sin, or whatever the imperfection or insecurity may be. This means you have to acknowledge it, expose it or call it what it is, agreeing with God that he can use it for his glory. Often this requires taking responsibility for your part in the equation and receiving God's forgiveness and forgiving yourself. If necessary, you might also need to forgive others who also bear responsibility. In the next chapter, we'll explore in more detail the healing work of forgiveness when you receive and release God's grace. For now, suffice it to say, I'm a living example of how God can flip the script in a person's life to show how his love, grace, and mercy can turn anyone's season around.

> **I'm a living example of how God can flip the script in a person's life to show how his love, grace, and mercy can turn anyone's season around.**

BEFORE AND AFTER

When I post photos on social media of myself when I was incarcerated, I'm not proud of my past. But I'm not embarrassed anymore either. I post those photos to show that I once was lost, but now I'm found. I was blind but now I see. I don't glory in my shame, but instead I seek to give God the glory for giving me new life in Christ. I was a dead man walking until Jesus cleansed me with the shedding of his sinless blood at Calvary. The words of 2 Corinthians 5:17 sum it up: "If anyone is in Christ, he is a new creation. The old has passed away; behold, the new has come." When you are willing to humbly reveal your scars, you give evidence of the life-changing transformation Jesus can make in a person's life. Skeptics might reject the claims of Christ, but they can't deny the authentic testimony of someone whose life has been changed by the power of the gospel. Seeing is believing when you reveal the scars of wounds God has healed in your life. So the next time you're inclined to post an old photo on social media for "Throwback Thursday," go ahead and share the difference Jesus has made in your life since that old photo was taken.

Don't ever underestimate the power of your "before and after" story of faith. God can take your story—the good, the bad, and the ugly—and use it to reveal his mighty power, amazing grace, and transforming love if you will let him. Are you trusting in God's promise in Romans 8:28? If so, then take some of those "all things" you might have tried to forget or deny because of shame or pain, and surrender them to God's purposes. Walk by faith, trusting in God's promise that he will bring good out of your situation, however bleak it may seem at the moment. Even when you can't see God at work in the midst of your circumstances, trust God's will for your life. And then by God's grace, move forward in the freedom you have in Christ, who makes all things new.

THE VOICE OF EXPERIENCE

Another important reason to reveal your scars is that it gives you authority to speak from your personal experiences of God's restoration and retooling of your life. My baseball coaches at every level had a huge impact on my career because they could always understand what I was going through. The reason I valued their insight and advice was because they were baseball players before they were coaches. We shared many similar experiences in the sport nostalgically known as "America's pastime."

Yes, modern analytics have changed real-time game strategies. Baseball gear is more sophisticated, and athletes are bigger, faster, and stronger. But the fundamentals of the sport haven't changed much since the first World Series was played in 1903 between the Boston Americans and Pittsburgh Pirates. My coaches had experienced the highs and lows of the game. They had endured batting slumps and persevered through losing streaks. They had also learned how to make the necessary adjustments to be successful in a sport that is as much mental as it is physical. In other words, since they had seen it, done it, and experienced it in the past, they could encourage and empower us in the present. The same is true along one's faith journey. In 2 Corinthians 1:3–5, Paul writes, "Blessed be the God and Father of our Lord Jesus Christ, the Father of mercies and God of all comfort, who comforts us in all our affliction, so that we may be able to comfort those who are in any affliction, with the comfort with which we ourselves are comforted by God. For as we share abundantly in Christ's sufferings, so through Christ we share abundantly in comfort too."

In other words, when you show your scars, you can tell others how God never leaves you nor forsakes you. Because you've experienced God's faithfulness in tough times, you can encourage those going through similar trials. As a former alcoholic and drug addict, I know what it's like to achieve sobriety only to relapse again and again. I've wrestled with self-loathing and shame. I understand the sense of rejection that casts a dark shadow over your life when you

Because you've experienced God's faithfulness in tough times, you can encourage those going through similar trials.

grow up with an absent father. I'm well acquainted with that empty feeling in the core of your being that only God can fill. I know what it's like to be financially and spiritually bankrupt. I've had cancer turn my life upside down twice. I've experienced the heartbreak of divorce and estrangement from my children. I've been incarcerated and humiliated for all the world to see. And in each of these afflictions, I have known the "God of all comfort." God's grace, mercy, and lovingkindness make me more than a survivor. I'm an overcomer in Jesus Christ. And the same God who delivered me from the depths of despair can do the same for anyone anywhere.

When you show your scars and tell your story of God's rescuing, redeeming, and restoring work in your life, you encourage those who are lonely and hurting by letting them know that what

God has done for you he can do for them. Psalm 147:3 declares, "He heals the brokenhearted and binds up their wounds."

THE BATTING CAGE

Seasons of suffering, heartache, and despair serve as God's batting cage for teaching you how to persevere, endure, and wait for his healing and deliverance. Let me explain. Baseball batting cages are typically a minimum of seventy feet long by fourteen feet wide by twelve feet high. A batting cage can seem like an extremely confining space when you compare it with a typical Major League Baseball park. Most open-air stadiums have at least 400 feet from home plate to the center field wall and 325 feet to 350 feet to the right field and left field walls. In the batting cage, a batter can't hit a 450-foot bomb to center field no matter how perfectly he times his swing and drives the bat through the baseball. The twelve-foot high net ceiling in the cage will quickly limit the baseball's ascent off the bat. Yet execute that swing in a baseball stadium, and prepare for fireworks. You see, the batting cage is where the batter perfects his swing, albeit in relative obscurity. And while the dimensions of the cage might seem limiting, the environment actually forces the batter to break down his swing and focus on the angles of his swinging motion and the placement of his head, shoulders, hips, and feet. A casual observer might think this type of exercise would be at best a waste of time based on the experience of a professional baseball player and at worst an insult to a professional's skill set. But in these moments in the batting cage, a batter is refining his craft, correcting bad habits, and reconnecting with the foundational techniques that make him successful come game time.

Similarly, God desires to use the limiting constraints of your pain and suffering to drive you to him and not away from him. When it seems that your prayers are bouncing off the ceiling like a baseball rebounding off the batting cage net, the reality is that God is closer to you than ever. Like a coach breaking down a batter's swing, God uses your trials to refocus your trust in him and realign your dependence on him. The closer you draw to God, the more aware you become of the things in your life that have come between you and your Creator. Then you can repent of your sin and by God's grace break the bad habits that have robbed you of the joy, peace, and contentment of living in Christ. If you were already walking closely with the Lord before your trial hit, then know that God doesn't waste anything in our lives. Don't waste your time asking God why. Ask your heavenly Father what he wants you to learn in the process.

In seasons when the world seems to be closing in on you, you can experience God as Psalm 46:1 describes him: "God is our refuge and strength, a very present help in trouble." You can't know God this way unless you go through stuff. And believe you me, trials and tribulations are a part of life. In fact, it's been said that everyone can be found in one of three seasons of life: in the midst of a trial, coming out of a trial, or awaiting a trial in the future. This is not a defeatist or pessimistic view of life. It's simply the reality of living in a fallen world. But the good news is, as I've been sharing throughout this book, God has prepared for us his spiritual RBIs—realities beyond imagination—which can equip us to live victoriously no matter what season of life we're in.

A PLAN FOR OUR SUFFERING

Embrace the apostle Paul's mindset of God's eternal purpose for your scars, as expressed in 2 Corinthians 4:16–18: "We do not lose heart. Though our outer self is wasting away, our inner self is being renewed day by day. For this light momentary affliction is preparing for us an eternal weight of glory beyond all comparison, as we look not to the things that are seen but to the things that are unseen. For the things that are seen are transient, but the things that are unseen are eternal."

From this passage, we can better understand God's plans for our suffering. When you pursue God's eternal purpose for your life, you realize that your external circumstances are a means to draw you closer to God. Through trials and pain, you have the opportunity to become more acutely aware of God's presence in your life. Then your scars aren't viewed as imperfections but instead as badges of honor—trophies of God's healing power and faithful promises like that in Philippians 4:19: "My God will supply every need of yours according to his riches in glory in Christ Jesus."

My mother died in 1995 from breast cancer at the young age

of fifty-five. She was a godly woman who loved Jesus with all her heart, soul, mind, and strength. She taught me to be kind and giving. My mother was a woman of prayer. After she died, I found her prayer journal under her bed. She had written a prayer for me: "God, knock him off his throne. Whatever you have to do, save him."

I miss my mother so much. She was my rock and foundation growing up in an unstable environment. She was the person I could count on and trust to be there for me and love me unconditionally. Most importantly, she prayed for my salvation until the Lord called her home. Although my mother's death continues to be a painful loss, her memory and legacy of faithfulness inspires me to never stop praying for God's will to be accomplished in my own children's lives. God's call on my life to share the life-changing message of the gospel with anybody anywhere is the answer to my mother's faithful and fervent prayers. She was never able to see the results of her prayers before she left this earth for her heavenly home. But I am living proof that God honored and answered her prayers. I hope my story encourages you to know that God is working in the middle of your situation even when you don't see any evidence of it. When the desired results you're praying for aren't yet in view, keep praying, trusting, and hoping that God will make a way where there seems to be no way. He is the Way Maker!

And when God doesn't answer your prayers according to

> **She had written a prayer for me: "God, knock him off his throne. Whatever you have to do, save him."**

your specific requests and timetable, trust that his plan is better—his realities for your life are beyond your imagination.

The apostle Paul seemed to have this perspective about his own chronic health condition. In describing his health issue as a "thorn in the flesh" from which he prayed to be delivered, Paul describes God's answer and his response in 2 Corinthians 12:9: "But He said to me, 'My grace is sufficient for you, for my power is made perfect in weakness.' Therefore I will boast all the more gladly of my weaknesses, so that the power of Christ may rest upon me."

When Paul writes about boasting in his weakness, he's not making excuses for his shortcomings or even seeking sympathy; he's just being real about life's struggles and challenges and how he depends on Jesus's enabling power to overcome his human limitations to accomplish God's purposes for his life. When we're honest and transparent about our imperfections and weaknesses, God delights in displaying his power through our limitations. When we acknowledge our weaknesses to God, we invite him to show off in our lives.

Someone once said that Christians are called to reflect God's glory in their lives like the moon reflects the sun. The moon is void of any source of energy to emanate light and brighten the night sky. Its radiant glow comes from reflecting the sun—the most powerful energy source in our solar system. Too often people try to live in their own strength and wisdom. But that's not where the true power source lies. God is glorified when we allow his power to shine through our scars.

THINK ABOUT IT

1. Consider "all" the things God works together for good. What situations are you trusting God to bring good out of?
2. How do Jesus's wounds heal us?
3. How was Jesus wounded for you?
4. What "scars" do you have? How do these reflect God's glory?
5. What sort of "before and after" story could you tell to show what God has done for you?
6. What "coaches" do you have in your life—people who share what they've learned through experience? Could you ever "coach" others in matters of faith?
7. How is God's power made perfect in your weakness?

RELEASE GOD'S GRACE

> If you forgive other people when they sin against you, your heavenly Father will also forgive you. But if you do not forgive others their sins, your Father will not forgive your sins.

MATTHEW 6:14–15 NIV

Another baseball analogy illustrates the game-changing power of grace and forgiveness. As a hitter, I would often foul off a pitch by swinging late and hitting the baseball into the stands behind home plate or somewhere else outside the field of play. Every time I did this, the umpire behind home plate would promptly replace the lost, used baseball by throwing the pitcher a brilliant white never-been-pitched baseball. Even though I was "at fault" for swinging late and hitting the foul ball out of play, the umpire graciously gave me another chance to hit the next pitch. The umpire essentially "forgave" my failure to keep the ball in play and instead replaced it himself. Furthermore, the new baseball had never been marred by the hit of another bat, soiled by the sweat of another player, or stained by the infield dirt or grassy outfield. In a small way, the foul ball scenario illustrates the forgiving, cleansing, justifying work Jesus does when he forgives our sin. Jesus not only doesn't hold our faults against us but also replaces our old, dirty, and worn out efforts with his pure and unstained righteousness. When we should be called out, dead in our sins, Jesus gives us new life in himself—a fresh start and new beginning.

The psalmist declares in Psalm 103:11–13,

As high as the heavens are above the earth,
> so great is his steadfast love toward those who fear him;
as far as the east is from the west,
> so far does he remove our transgressions from us.

As a father shows compassion to his children,
> so the LORD shows compassion to those who fear him.

During my Major League Baseball career, I played for the Mets and Yankees on the East Coast and Dodgers and Giants on the West Coast. These cross-country teams are located nearly three thousand miles apart. When God forgives us of our sins, he separates them from us as far as the East Coast is from the West Coast—and even farther. Get the picture?

Micah 7:19 declares that God buries our sin in "the depths of the sea." Jeremiah 31:34 reminds us that upon confessing our sins to God in repentance, he will "remember [our] sin no more." He expunges them from our record as if they had never occurred. When God calls me to heaven, my obituary will likely recount my success as a professional baseball player and failures in life outside the sport. All-Star Awards and World Series championships will be listed alongside my criminal convictions for federal tax evasion, cocaine possession, and probation violation. But when my heavenly

When my heavenly Father looks at me, he doesn't keep score of my good and bad days on or off the field.

Father looks at me, he doesn't keep score of my good and bad days on or off the field. When I stand before God to give an account for my life like everyone will do when they die, I will claim the shed blood of Jesus for the forgiveness of my sins. And because I uncover my sins by confessing them to God, he covers them with the sinless blood of his Son. But for those who choose to cover their sins before God and not repent before they die, he will uncover their sins with his judgment.

AMBASSADORS

You might be thinking, didn't we unpack forgiveness already with the spiritual RBI in chapter 1, called "Receive God's Grace"? Yes, we did. Forgive me for being a little redundant, but the reason I'm belaboring the point here is to remind us that without God's forgiveness, we can't be made right with him. In chapter 2, I addressed the second spiritual RBI, called "Redefine Your Identity," where we recognized that God calls those who have received his forgiveness to help reconcile those to God who still need to receive his forgiveness. God didn't just save you and me from our sins for our sake. He saved you and me from our sins so that we might also help others discover the grace of God's forgiveness for themselves. That's why Scripture calls Christians ambassadors for Christ.

A baseball game's statistical chart, also known as the box score, often shows the winning team with at least twice as many hits as runs. That's because runs are most often scored when batters advance runners on the bases through a succession of hits. Similarly, think of the exponential effect when one of Christ's ambassadors helps lead someone else to receive God's forgiveness, who then helps lead someone else to receive God's forgiveness, and so on. The difference, spiritually speaking, is not the equivalent of just piling up base hits—it's multiplying home runs for the kingdom of God!

That's what is so beautiful about the power of forgiveness— it's more caught than taught. When someone truly experiences forgiveness by placing their faith in Jesus Christ's sacrificial death on the cross and miraculous resurrection from the grave, they can't help but forgive others, as well as seek others' forgiveness. That's the ripple effect of the miracle of forgiveness.

A heart of forgiveness does not come naturally. Forgiveness

is God's idea, not ours. Forgiveness comes from the Spirit of God living inside you. It's the main reason God sent Jesus to earth—to give us victory over sin and the grave through his forgiveness. Your willingness to forgive others and seek others' forgiveness are evidence that you trust in the finished work of Christ on the cross.

Think of the shape of the cross. One piece of wood is vertical and the other is horizontal. The vertical dimension of the cross symbolizes our relationship with God. God spared nothing—not even the death of his perfect and sinless Son—so that we could be forgiven. Likewise, since we have received God's forgiveness by no merit of our own, is there any offense or sin against us that we shouldn't be willing to forgive? Notice here that I used the word *willing* and not *able*. God just needs our willingness to forgive, and then he will equip, empower, and enable us with his Spirit of forgiveness. The horizontal dimension of the cross represents our relationships with others. If Jesus, who is sinless, can forgive us, then shouldn't we, who are sinners, be able to forgive fellow sinners? Remember what Jesus said from the cross: "Father, forgive them, for they know not what they do" (Luke 23:34).

RIGHT RELATIONSHIP

We can't be in a right relationship with God if we aren't in a right relationship with others. Matthew 6:14–15 (NIV) states this clearly: "If you forgive other people when they sin against you, your heavenly Father will also forgive you. But if you do not forgive others their sins, your Father will not forgive your sins" God convicted me of this reality several years ago when he told me to seek reconciliation with my father. But catch this: God didn't tell me to forgive my father; he told me to go ask my father to forgive me.

I was in San Diego to preach at a men's conference when my brother called to say that our father had suffered a stroke and was hospitalized nearby. My heart immediately came under the conviction of the Holy Spirit. How could I preach

God didn't tell me to forgive my father; he told me to go ask my father to forgive me.

before a large group of men about experiencing my heavenly Father's loving forgiveness while at the same time being estranged from my earthly father? How could I talk about the life-changing power of receiving God's grace and forgiveness of my sins if I wasn't willing to release or share God's grace with the one person in the world who had hurt me most?

You might think the most reasonable path to reconciling with my father would have been to muster the courage to offer him forgiveness for abusing and abandoning me and my family. Now that I had accepted God's forgiveness for my own sins and shortcomings, I should certainly be able to extend forgiveness to him. But it was more complicated than that.

Growing up in a dysfunctional single-parent family had set me on a path of destruction that nearly killed me. Years earlier, my father had visited me at the Betty Ford Center in Southern

California, where I was going through rehabilitation for my drug and alcohol addiction. At that point he had the opportunity to own his mistakes and seek my forgiveness, but he didn't. Instead, he denied any recollection of being verbally or physically abusive. The pain of that day was like pouring salt on the gaping wound that was my broken heart.

So this time the Spirit gave me a new approach. I asked my father to forgive me.

That's right. Instead of offering him my forgiveness, I asked for his. I confessed that I had vindictively kept him at a distance throughout my professional baseball career and adult life. Would he, could he, forgive me?

Then something miraculous happened. He immediately said he would forgive me. I broke down weeping as I laid my face across his lap. A flood of emotion poured out of me, as if a dam had burst. Sobbing, I said, "I'm sorry, I was wrong. Forgive me, please. The Lord changed my life. Would you like to experience that?"

And then another miracle happened. My father said yes! As he lay in his hospital bed, my father prayed with me and asked God to forgive him of his sins. Then he trusted in Jesus as his Savior and Lord. Immediately after that prayer with my father, I felt like a ton of bricks had been lifted from my shoulders. This reconciliation with my father reminded me of the moment I first accepted Jesus as my Savior and Lord while crying uncontrollably at that stadium crusade in Anaheim in 1991.

My father died about six months after my bedside visit at

the San Diego area hospital. I am so thankful God gave me the opportunity to lead my father to Jesus before he passed away. But that would never have happened if I had not first willingly answered God's call to humbly ask for my father's forgiveness. In that act, I owned up to my unwillingness to forgive him, an attitude I had clung to for so many years. And in that moment of personal reconciliation, I became an ambassador of Christ's reconciliation.

Little did I know at the time how freeing and liberating this experience would be for me. Forgiving my father and receiving his forgiveness set me free of emotional bondage that had dominated my life. It's been said that unforgiveness is like drinking poison and hoping the other person dies. That's an apt description of much of my life. But reconciliation with God and with my father changed that. Quoting the late theologian Lewis Smedes, "To forgive is to set a prisoner free and discover that the prisoner was you."

FORGIVING YOURSELF

Another important aspect of forgiveness that can easily be overlooked is the need to forgive yourself. I believe this is where Satan does some of his most crippling work. The Enemy loves to whisper in your ear and daily remind you of your past sins, mistakes, and failures. God's Word calls the devil a liar, deceiver, thief, and murderer. His primary mission is to rob Christ followers of their joy, peace, and purpose. If Satan can get you to camp out in the land of regret and remorse, then you can't be much of an ambassador for Christ. It's impossible to live victoriously in Christ while wallowing in shame and self-pity. When you're focused on your past, you can't fix your eyes on God's vision for your future or recognize the opportunities in front of you to serve and encourage others. When you're mired in your mistakes, you can't move forward to accomplish all the good works God has prepared for you to do. And that's precisely Satan's agenda. He wants to make you feel inferior, inadequate, unqualified. I'll state it a different way than previously: God doesn't work through people who are qualified; he qualifies people for his work. *And the way God qualifies those on his team is through his rescuing, redeeming, and restoring work in their lives.*

To release God's grace by forgiving others, you must first receive God's forgiveness and then forgive yourself. Think about it this way: If God can forgive us, then who are we to refuse to forgive ourselves? If you're struggling to forgive yourself, then it begs the question of whether you have first received God's forgiveness. Again, forgiving yourself isn't easy. That's why God didn't leave us to ourselves to make it happen. He first forgave us and promised us a helper in the person of the Holy Spirit, who is able to guide and direct us in righteousness. The next time Satan reminds you of your past, and he will, remind him that he is a liar and deceiver and that your heavenly Father has cast your sins as far as the east is from the west. And furthermore, while you're at it, go ahead and claim God's promise in Isaiah 54:17:

"No weapon that is fashioned against you shall succeed,
    and you shall refute every tongue that rises against you
      in judgment.
This is the heritage of the servants of the LORD
    and their vindication from me," declares the LORD.

I claim this promise every time Satan tries to distract and discourage me from running the race God has set before me.

FAMILY MATTERS

Forgiving myself has enabled me to pursue thriving and healthy relationships with each of my four daughters and two sons. They're all adults now, in their twenties and thirties, but for seasons of their childhood, I wasn't engaged in their lives, providing the nurturing support and godly example a father should. I provided for their material and physical needs, but I failed miserably in helping to meet their emotional and spiritual needs. I have since reconciled with each of my children. When I sought their forgiveness, I did so by owning my failures. I didn't make excuses by blaming my father for his poor example or using my seasons of drug addiction as an explanation for shutting them out of my life. I told them I was sorry for my self-centeredness and selfishness and for failing to make my relationship with them a priority. And I'm humbled to say that they all have graciously forgiven me for my shortcomings as their father.

I can't emphasize enough the importance of the child-parent relationship. The majority of dysfunction that is running rampant in America today stems from broken families. In the book of Genesis, we are taught that God created male and female and told them to procreate and raise a family as husband and wife. He appointed husbands and fathers to be the spiritual leaders of their families by setting a godly example of selfless, loving servanthood. The ultimate purpose of a father is to model the attributes of God to his children so they can better understand how much their heavenly Father loves and cares for them. Proverbs 22:6 states, "Train up a child in the way he should go; even when he is old he will not depart from it." I'm living proof of the power of this promise. No, my father wasn't a part of this process, but my mother was. Even in the toxic environment of our home, she did her best to teach her children biblical principles. Though my father's failure to be a godly example and spiritual leader in our home undermined my mother's words of wisdom, she always told me that God loved me and had a purpose for my life.

For better or worse, the foundation or lack thereof established in the home often dictates a child's future. God entrusts parents to care for the souls of his precious children. This is a tremendous burden on my heart as I watch the cycle of dysfunction and brokenness continue to show itself through addictions, adulteries, and broken marriages. The next generation of young people are starving for a healing they don't even know they need. Please hear me from a place of hope and not judgment. Although I never physically abused my children, I projected the same dysfunctional pattern on them that I experienced as a kid growing up in Los Angeles.

Training children in the way they should go starts with understanding them. God has hardwired all of us with certain personalities. With loving attention, parents can help their children discover their own talents and passions and how to use them for God's purposes. Deuteronomy 6:5–7 states, "You shall love the LORD your God with all your heart and with all your soul and with all your might. And these words that I command you today shall be on your heart. You shall teach them diligently to your children, and shall talk of them when you sit in your house, and when you walk by the way, and when you lie down, and when you rise."

Yes, parents should meet the physical and emotional needs of their children and provide a safe and nurturing environment for them to thrive. But more important than a parent's ability to provide their child with a college education or financial inheritance is God's Word, which commands parents to teach and train their children in biblical principles. When parents faithfully teach their children the Word of God, it is one of the most grace-filled gifts they could ever give them. And because the Bible is living and active, it is a gift that keeps on giving throughout one's lifetime.

Divorce, abuse, and neglect tear apart the hearts of our children. I experienced it, and maybe you have too. I believe with all my heart that marriage and parenting should carry the highest level of responsibility in society. More importantly, I contend that if Christian homes returned to the foundation of God's Word, revival and spiritual awakening would spread across America like fans doing the wave across a baseball stadium. In Ephesians 5:25–33, we see God's instructions for a grace-filled marriage that showcases the gospel to a family, community, state, nation, and world:

> Husbands, love your wives, as Christ loved the church and gave himself up for her, that he might sanctify her, having cleansed her by the washing of water with the word, so that he might present the church to himself in splendor, without spot or wrinkle or any such thing, that she might be holy and without blemish. In the same way husbands should love their wives as their own bodies. He who loves his wife loves himself. For no one ever hated his own flesh, but nourishes and cherishes it, just as Christ does the church, because we are members of his body. "Therefore a man shall leave his father and mother and hold fast to his wife, and the two shall become one flesh." This mystery is profound, and I am saying that it refers to Christ and the church. However, let each one of you love his wife as himself, and let the wife see that she respects her husband.

A husband and wife experience a great marriage when they are centered on the ways of God. Their love comes from their submission to the heart of God, which loves beyond emotions, self-pleasures, and desires. A grace-filled marriage is one in which a husband and wife are quick to forgive each other and intentional in putting the other's needs before their own. They love each other selflessly and serve each other tirelessly. A mom and dad who love each other this way make great parents and also showcase the gospel to their children. When children see their parents readily admitting when they are wrong, they in turn learn how to release God's grace by forgiving one another. A husband who loves his wife as Christ loves the church and a wife who honors and respects the servant leadership of her husband both display the biblical model for a healthy and fulfilling marriage.[1] Parents who lead and raise their children according to the ways of God understand that fathers and mothers are responsible for helping shape how their children perceive the world and discern what is true. Some of the greatest parental advice I have found in Scripture is Proverbs 9:10: "The fear of the LORD is the beginning of wisdom, and the knowledge of the Holy One is insight." Children are a matchless gift from God. He expects us to care for this great gift by raising them according to his instruction manual for life, the Bible.

THE MAN IN THE MIRROR

What I've written about my father is in no way intended disrespectfully. I point to this scar of mine only to convey a simple reality: hurt people hurt people, especially the ones they love most. The beatings, critical words, and emotional abuse from my father broke me as a person. This hindered me from knowing how to become a true man of God. It stunted my emotional and spiritual growth. My father did not surrender to God and therefore never knew the love and healing power of his heavenly Father until shortly before he died. God calls us to embrace his ways of living and to model them for our children. This is the answer to the drug epidemic, the divorce rate, and the growing incarcerated population in our world today.

My father came from serious abuse and neglect. I swore I would never be like him! Then one day I looked at myself in the mirror and saw a vision of my father staring me right in the face. The same pattern of abuse and neglect was continuing in me. I finally realized I had to make a choice. I said to myself, "Darryl, are you going to choose to surrender to God and fight to get well? Are you going to get the help you need and break the cycle of dysfunction in your family once and for all?"

Hurt people hurt people, especially the ones they love most.

My answer was a profound *yes*! I finally acknowledged that if nothing changes, well then, nothing changes. Life change begins inside the person who chooses to surrender to God and participate in his transforming process. I couldn't change my past, but God could change how I allowed my past to shape the present and influence my future.

Some of you reading this book need to make this same choice. Will you choose God and his ways or continue on the same dead-end road? Maybe you're already making a U-turn in life. Reading this book is a hopeful start. If you have a genuine desire to turn your season around, God will walk alongside you every step of the way. Follow God's commands and claim the promises from his Word, and see what God does.

You're probably familiar with the adage that a chain is only as strong as its weakest link. This axiom applies to nearly any type of organization, including churches, sports teams, and families. But have you ever thought of the spiritual implications of this truism? When King Solomon dedicated the temple to God, as recorded in 2 Chronicles 7:14, God promised the Israelites a conditional blessing: " If my people who are called by my name humble themselves, and pray and seek my face and turn from their wicked ways, then I will hear from heaven and will forgive their sin and heal their land."

In this timeless promise from the Word of God, the people of God are assured healing when they humbly seek God's forgiveness. Do you see the power of forgiveness in this promise? Yes, the promise of healing is predicated on God's people—not unbelievers—repenting of their wicked ways. As liberating and freeing as forgiveness can be for those who are willing to receive and release God's grace, the opposite is also true for those who aren't willing to forgive or turn from their wicked ways. In other words, one's unwillingness to receive or release forgiveness could be the very thing that blocks God's healing for them and the ones they love. Let's not be the reason for God's withholding his blessings of healing for his people and this world because we weren't willing to forgive ourselves or someone else. God forbid we become the weakest link that holds back God's favor and wonder-working power in his church throughout the world. As humans, we don't live our lives in a vacuum. One of the many lessons we've learned from the COVID-19 global pandemic is that everything everybody does has implications for everyone else—directly or indirectly. One of the biggest lies in our culture today is that an individual should be able to do whatever he or she desires so long as it doesn't hurt or infringe on the rights of someone else. The fact of the matter is that everything we do or fail to do affects someone else at some level, either positively or negatively. More importantly, as Christ followers faithfully seek God through prayer and Bible study—and in turn love, forgive, and serve others—then those who don't know Jesus as their Savior and Lord will increasingly be drawn to faith in him by the power of our testimonies of his irresistible grace.

THINK ABOUT IT

1. How would you define forgiveness?
2. When have you needed to ask for forgiveness, or to forgive someone else?
3. What damage is caused by grudge holding—when people refuse to ask for forgiveness or grant it? Have you ever experienced this?
4. Consider the image of the cross, with its vertical and horizontal pieces. What does that mean to you?

5. How can parents teach their children about forgiveness?
6. If hurt people hurt people, do forgiven people forgive people? Have you seen either of these statements prove true?
7. What could you do differently in your life to become an ambassador of Christ's reconciliation?

REFLECT GOD'S HEART

> You are a chosen race, a royal priesthood, a holy nation, a people for his own possession, that you may proclaim the excellencies of him who called you out of darkness into his marvelous light. Once you were not a people, but now you are God's people; once you had not received mercy, but now you have received mercy.
>
> 1 PETER 2:9–10

During the regular season, a Major League Baseball team can have twenty-five players on their active roster. That number can grow to as many as forty players for the playoffs and the World Series championship run. At any point in a game, however, only nine fielders can play at once or make up the batting order. But make no mistake, every player on the active roster is crucial to a team's success, and they aren't there by accident. Each player's skill set has been vetted by professional baseball scouts from elite development and instruction leagues to the three-tier minor league system. Major League Baseball has a talent pipeline filled with hundreds of players all competing for the chance to showcase their skills in big league stadiums teeming with tens of thousands of fans.

From the players who start nearly every game, to those who come off the bench at a moment's notice, to the pitcher who toes the rubber every fifth game, to the pinch hitter, runner, and relief pitcher, every player on the roster has a significant role to play in the team's success. And if a player is not ready to perform at his highest level when the manager calls his number, another player is waiting in line to take his place. In fact, a benefit to having extra players on the roster is that whenever a player is struggling, another player can step in and contribute.

That happened to me in game six of the 1986 World Series against the Boston Red Sox. Mets manager Davey Johnson benched me for Lee Mazzilli late in the game because I had been struggling to produce at the plate. I didn't take too kindly to being replaced, but it certainly motivated me for game seven, when I hit a towering solo home run over the right field wall in Shea Stadium. I'm not proud to say I barely jogged around the bases, going as slowly as possible, to protest my manager's decision to take me out of the lineup in game six. Hall of Fame broadcaster Vin Scully mocked me on the national television broadcast by suggesting it could take twenty minutes to complete my home run parade. When I finally reached home plate, I was met by Mets veteran third baseman and eventual World Series MVP Ray Knight, who promptly told me to quit pouting and apologize to my manager for caring more about myself than the team. When you spend nine months out of the year with your teammates and coaches traveling around the country and battling together nearly every day in pursuit of a championship, you become like a family. Players encourage one another and hold each other accountable.

When I hit that home run in game seven to extend our game-winning lead to two runs, Mets fans roared in applause, but I couldn't fully enjoy the moment because I was bitter and had a vengeful spirit toward my manager. Despite my success, I was still not content. You see, during that season of my life I couldn't reflect God's heart because I had not yet exchanged my heart for his. But God, in his master plan, unbeknownst to me at the time, was sowing seeds of the gospel into my heart through the daily example of beloved Mets catcher and field general Gary Carter.

THE KID

Nicknamed "Kid," Gary had already played eleven seasons with the Montreal Expos before he joined the Mets in 1985. He had earned his nickname because he played every game with the joyful enthusiasm of a kid in a candy store. Our baseball careers had similar beginnings. We are both from California. He finished second in Rookie of the Year voting in 1975 as a twenty-one-year-old All-Star outfielder. By the time we teamed up a decade later, Carter was already a seven-time All-Star. And while we both enjoyed tremendous individual and team success as teammates for five seasons, Gary's life trajectory off the field couldn't have been more different from mine.

You see, Gary didn't just love playing the game of baseball. He loved Jesus with all his heart, soul, mind, and strength. I can't remember a time when I didn't see Gary smiling from ear to ear, regardless of how he or the team was performing. The joy of the Lord and the peace that passes understanding were all over Gary. He was such an encourager to me and everyone on the team.

Gary loved his wife and children. After our out-of-town games, he always returned to the team hotel, while I and most of our teammates headed to the bars and strip clubs. Gary put God first in his life, his family second, and baseball was a distant third. But interestingly, Gary never judged me or condemned me for my self-centered ways. He always told me that God had a great plan for my life that was bigger than my fleeting baseball career.

Gary wasn't preachy; he was sincere and genuine. His life consistently exuded grace and compassion. He had a zest for life like I've seen in very few people. And in my opinion, he's the primary reason the Mets won the 1986 World Series.

It was Gary's two-out single in the bottom of the tenth inning with the bases empty in game six that ignited our improbable comeback from a two-run deficit to force a game seven. After the comeback win, Gary said his mindset going to bat with two outs in the bottom of the tenth inning had been simply not to go down in history as making the last out in the World Series. His base hit to left field was followed by a single from Kevin Mitchell. And then Ray Knight singled as Gary raced home from second base to cut the deficit to one run. Mitchell scored the tying run from third base on a wild pitch. Then Red Sox first baseman Bill Buckner watched Mookie Wilson's routine ground ball roll between his legs.

Everyone remembers Buckner's infamous error allowing Knight to score the game-winning run. Most people forget that Gary Carter had tied that game with a sacrifice fly in the bottom of the eighth inning, besides starting the tenth-inning rally. Then in the deciding game seven, Gary again drove in the tying run in the sixth inning before I later homered to extend our lead en route to our victory—and the second World Series championship in the history of the Mets' storied franchise. Gary also homered twice over the Green Monster at Boston's Fenway Park in game four and totaled nine RBIs for the World Series.

By the end of his nineteen-year career with the Expos, Mets, Giants, and Dodgers, Gary had amassed 324 home runs, 1,225 RBIs, and a .262 batting average. During his eleven All-Star Game appearances, he was selected twice as the MVP. And he holds the distinction of being the only player to hit two home runs in an All-Star Game and a World Series game. It should come as no surprise that after retiring in 1992, Gary was elected into the Major League Baseball Hall of Fame in 2003. His bronze plaque in Cooperstown, New York, reads: "An exuberant on-field general with a signature smile who was known for clutch hitting and rock-solid defense over 19 seasons."[1]

But I'll always remember Gary most importantly for his humility and the way he modeled how to reflect God's heart day in and day out.

On February 16, 2012, God called Gary to his heavenly home after a battle with brain cancer. He was only fifty-seven years young when he died. But the life he lived, he maximized for God's glory. At the news of Gary's passing, the Mets organization issued the following press statement: "He did everything with enthusiasm and with gusto on and off the field. His smile was infectious. He guided our young pitching staff to the World Series title in 1986 and he devoted an equal amount of time and energy raising awareness for a multitude of charities and community causes. He was a Hall of Famer in everything he did."[2]

But the best tribute to Gary's life was written by his daughter Kimmy on the family website. "I am deeply saddened to tell you all that my precious dad went to be with Jesus today at 4:10 p.m. This is the most difficult thing I have ever had to write in my entire life, but I wanted you all to know. He is in Heaven and has reunited with his mom and dad. I believe with all my heart that dad had a STANDING OVATION as he walked through the gates of Heaven to be with Jesus."[3]

I can think of no greater legacy to leave for your children than the gift of knowing that their father or mother stored up "treasures in heaven, where neither moth nor rust destroys and where thieves do not break in and steal" (Matthew 6:20). Personally, I would trade every award and accolade I ever received from the game of baseball to know that my children, family, and friends would one day be reunited with me in heaven. I praise the Lord for Gary's consistent example of how to reflect God's heart as a man of God. My only regret is that I didn't follow his example sooner. I plead with you right now, don't delay in responding to God's invitation to turn your season around. God can do better than the Mets' World Series comeback miracle; he can do a miracle in the life of anyone who turns to him through faith in Jesus Christ.

I'll say it again: God is still in the rescuing, redeeming, and restoring business. He can rescue you from your pit, redeem you from your predicament, and restore you with his promises. To put it another way, God's heart is to save you from your sins because he loves you. You are then able to tell other sinners how they can enjoy his forgiveness and promise of eternal life in heaven.

God has done exactly that in my life, and he can do it in your life as well.

A GRATEFUL HEART

In 1 Peter 2:9–10, quoted at the top of this chapter, we see a picture of our relationship with God—and a sense of his heart. He called us "out of darkness into his marvelous light."

It's important that we never forget where we came from. I'm not advocating that we live in the past. I am saying that by remembering who you were before Christ stepped into your life, you will be less likely to take his grace and mercy for granted. Consequently, a heart of gratefulness will help you rejoice in the Lord always. The lyrics of an old hymn say it well:

> Count your many blessings, name them one by one,
> And it will surprise you what the Lord has done.

If I'm going to talk about my baseball career, how much more should I talk about God's mercy, grace, and goodness in my life! The Bible says you and I were groping in spiritual darkness, walking blindly like sheep without a shepherd. Then Jesus, the Light of the World, stepped into our darkness—and the darkness fled like roaches when you flip on the light switch. Jesus came looking for you and me. We didn't go looking for Jesus. The Bible says before Jesus changed our hearts and appetites, our bellies were our gods and all we cared about was satisfying our fleshly desires. It does not come naturally to hunger and thirst for God, but that's the new heart he gives us.

The 1 Peter passage goes on to say, "Once you were not a people, but now you are God's people" (v. 10). God's amazing grace has granted us not just forgiveness but also adoption into the family of God. And when Christ followers are adopted into God's family, they join a royal priesthood.

Before Christ came to earth, the Israelite priests represented the people before God. But when Christ came, he made a way through the cross for people to have direct access to God. And now, as part of Jesus's royal priesthood, lovers of God are called to minister in Jesus's name for the glory of God. Let's not forget that the 1 Peter 2 passage also describes Christians as "a people for his own possession" (v. 9). We have been bought with the blood of Christ, and now we belong to him. Once we were slaves to sin, but now we serve Christ in righteousness. That is what reflecting God's heart means.

A "SET-APART" HEART

Looking back on my baseball career, I now see some parallels to the big idea of being set apart with a special calling similar to that of a royal priesthood.

As part of a Major League Baseball team, players are set apart from the fans. I dressed and acted differently inside the baseball park. My teammates, coaches, and I shared a language unique to our circumstances. We followed a set of rules that governed our actions. We had contracts that stipulated our payment or rewards based on fulfilled expectations and commitments. And after every game, we were invited to tell our story and explain our actions as television, radio, newspaper, and digital media reporters asked questions on behalf of inquiring minds around the world.

Similarly, when you are part of God's family, or his royal

priesthood, you are set apart from those who have not been adopted into God's family. You are to be holy because your God is holy. You no longer know God only as your Creator but also as your heavenly Father, Savior, and Lord. You have been clothed in the righteousness of God instead of the condemnation of your sins. Your speech and actions are to be marked by holiness, grace mercy, compassion, and purity. Your code of conduct is firmly established in the laws of God. And while your value is measured by God's immeasurable love, his promises of blessing are conditional on your faithfulness and obedience to your eternal Owner, Master, Boss, Commander, Defender, Justifier, King, Savior and Lord. And God's Word commands his children to always be ready to give an answer for the hope that lies within them.

The family of God, or priesthood of believers, is called to work together like a team as well. In 1 Corinthians 12:12, the apostle Paul likens the church to how God designed the human body to work: "Just as the body is one and has many members, and all the members of the body, though many, are one body, so it is with Christ." Notice that God's Word uses the human body as an analogy for the church. Let's camp out on this idea for a minute.

The wonder of God's creation is seen every time he fashions a person in their mother's womb. The human body is a miraculous synchronization of intricately designed systems—including skeletal, muscular, nervous, respiratory, and circulatory—that interdependently coexist. Each part of the body has a specific and necessary function. When this delicate balance gets out of sync, we struggle to function at optimal efficiency.

I know all about that. As a professional athlete, I depended on my body being strong and healthy to compete at the highest level. But over the course of my career, I sustained a number of injuries that required surgery and rehabilitation. Early in my career with the Mets, I tore ligaments in my right thumb diving to catch a ball near the right field foul line in Shea Stadium against the Philadelphia Phillies. The ground didn't give up any territory when I jammed my glove-covered thumb into the turf. You could say I won the battle by catching the ball, but I lost the war, being sidelined for six weeks after surgery. I must admit I never thought much about my thumb contributing significantly to my performance on the baseball field until I couldn't swing a bat or catch a fly ball with the appendage in a splint.

In another game against the Phillies in 1993, on a cold, damp night in Philadelphia, I ruptured a disc in my lower back while scoring from second base. Those who have experienced herniated, bulging, or slipped discs understand all too well how excruciatingly painful it can be when a disc in your back that is out of alignment pinches your sciatic nerve. It took me about three years to fully recover from my back injury and subsequent surgery, which explains the sharp decline in my batting production during my following seasons with the Dodgers. In 1997 I played in only eleven games with the Yankees due to a left knee injury that was the cumulative effect of sliding for more than two hundred stolen bases in my career. Furthermore, my left knee always took the weight of my swing as my left leg anchored my batting stance. All that to say, when my body broke down physically, my effectiveness on the field diminished significantly.

It's the same way with Jesus's church, also called the body of Christ. Every member of God's family plays a vital role in sharing and showing the love of Christ. Jesus's love for his church is undeniable. He died for his church. He built his church. And he is coming back for his church like a bridegroom longing for his bride. But until Christ returns, he is testing the sincerity of his bride's faith through trials, like a goldsmith refining and purifying the elements through fire. First Peter 1:3–9 states it better than I can:

> Blessed be the God and Father of our Lord Jesus Christ! According to his great mercy, he has caused us to be born again to a living hope through the resurrection of Jesus Christ from the dead, to an inheritance that is imperishable, undefiled, and unfading, kept in heaven for you, who by God's power are being guarded through faith for a salvation ready to be revealed in the last time. In this you rejoice, though now for a little while, if necessary, you have been grieved by various trials, so that the tested genuineness of your faith— more precious than gold that perishes though it is tested by fire—may be found to result in praise and glory and honor at the revelation of Jesus Christ. Though you have not seen him, you love him. Though you do not now see him, you believe in him and rejoice with joy that is inexpressible and

filled with glory, obtaining the outcome of your faith, the salvation of your souls.

Those who are part of God's family look forward to an eternity free of sin, sickness, heartbreak, and suffering. In the meantime, however, Christ followers have been called and equipped to live victoriously even in the midst of a sin-stained and disease-ridden world that is perishing day by day.

A FAITHFUL HEART

The ability to reflect God's heart in any circumstance is a supernatural response birthed out of the Holy Spirit's presence in your life. If you have been adopted into the family of God by grace through faith in Jesus Christ, then the Holy Spirit has taken residence in your heart, soul, mind, and body. If that's your reality, the question should never be how much of the Holy Spirit do you have but instead how much of you does the Holy Spirit have? Are you yielding to the prompting, leading, and directing of the Holy Spirit in your life?

The question should never be how much of the Holy Spirit do you have but instead how much of you does the Holy Spirit have?

A good way to evaluate how you are appropriating the power of the Holy Spirit in your life is by measuring your level of contentment, even in the face of difficulties. In Philippians 4:11–13, the apostle Paul sets the gold standard for an attitude of gratitude: "I have learned in whatever situation I am to be content. I know how to be brought low, and I know how to abound. In any and every circumstance, I have learned the secret of facing plenty and hunger, abundance and need. I can do all things through him who strengthens me."

How can Paul say this? Because he has had a lot of practice enduring dangerous and painful seasons of life. In 2 Corinthians 11 he mentions five occasions when he was whipped with thirty-nine lashes. He was beaten three times with rods and stoned once. Paul was shipwrecked three times and adrift at sea for more than twenty-four hours. And in every perilous situation, he says that his relationship with Christ alone was enough for him to persevere and overcome his despair.

Paul's declaration that he can do anything with Christ's help is often quoted to support someone's aspirational goals or dreams, but taken in context, it carries a slightly different meaning. His declaration that he can do anything with Christ's strength is less about Christ empowering him to achieve his goals and more about Christ enabling him to endure whatever challenges come his way for the cause of Christ.

As our culture becomes increasingly secular and biblically illiterate, those who stand on God's Word will be ridiculed and persecuted. Jesus warned his followers not to be surprised when the world hated them, because they had hated him first: "If the world hates you, know that it has hated me before it hated you. If you were of the world, the world would love you as its own;

but because you are not of the world, but I chose you out of the world, therefore the world hates you" (John 15:18–19).

When I was living by the world's standards, I was insanely popular. Before the advent of social media, I had throngs of followers everywhere I went. When I paid the tab for everyone in the bar to celebrate a late-night victory after a ballgame, everybody wanted to be my friend. Even when I dislocated my shoulder in my first season with my hometown Dodgers, an injury that kept me on the bench for the first half of the season, I was still one of the leading vote recipients for the All-Star Game—a testament to my popularity rather than my production.

But it's a different story today. The overwhelming majority of Americans reject my biblical worldview. According to a 2020 survey conducted by the Cultural Research Center at Arizona Christian University, only 6 percent of Americans hold a biblical worldview. (In short, a biblical worldview is defined as a belief system informed and guided by the Holy Bible, resulting in convictions, actions, and choices that are consistent with what the Bible teaches. In other words, a biblical worldview is held when someone chooses to see, interpret, and discern truth about the world's past, present, and future in light of God's Word and then act according to biblical precepts.)

The report, called the American Worldview Inventory, led by veteran researcher George Barna, analyzed survey responses from one thousand telephone interviews and another one thousand online questionnaires. With fifty-one questions about what people believe and how they act on those beliefs, the survey found that only about 20 percent of those who said they attended evangelical Protestant churches espoused a biblical worldview. Just 16 percent of those who attended charismatic or Pentecostal churches ascribed to a biblical worldview, while mainline Protestants were at 8 percent and Catholics at 1 percent.[4]

The survey also revealed that Americans who identify as Christian but don't profess to know Christ personally as their Savior represent 54 percent of the US population. And of that sector of the population, only one-tenth of 1 percent hold a biblical worldview. Barna reported that his broader worldview research among the American population consistently shows that the predominant values in the United States today include happiness, freedom, expression, experiences, entitlement, entertainment, control, comfort, and acceptance. Where is "dying to self" and "living for Christ" expressed in these modern American values? How do these priorities align with the Bible's teaching to present your body as a living sacrifice, holy and acceptable to God as your spiritual act of worship? I contend that the biblical values of sacrifice, selflessness, and humility reflect God's heart and contrast sharply with the cultural values prevalent in our world today.

> **The biblical values of sacrifice, selflessness, and humility reflect God's heart and contrast sharply with the cultural values prevalent in our world today.**

A HEART THAT REJECTS PRIDE

Major League Baseball is governed by an almost-two-hundred-page rule book. But it's the unwritten rules of baseball that reveal the acceptable code of conduct, values, and attitudes that define the game. Let me give you an insider's perspective on what type of behavior by a hitter is considered disrespectful of the opposing pitcher.

Number one, don't gaze or stare admiringly at your home run.

Number two, tossing or flipping the bat after crushing the baseball is considered belittling a pitcher.

Number three, don't ever attempt a bunt to break up a no-hitter.

Number four, avoid swinging at a 3–0 pitch or stealing a base when your team has a big lead.

In general, you want to avoid actions that could be interpreted as upstaging your opponent or "piling on," so to speak. Violate the hitter's rules of etiquette and the next time you step inside the batter's box, expect to be served a ninety-five-mile-per-hour fastball under your chin or at your backside.

Now, before you become too judgmental about the game of baseball, consider that in the game of life, just as in baseball, pride is the common denominator that trips us up.

The godly wisdom of Proverbs 16:18–25 provides the antidote to pride's poison:

> Pride goes before destruction,
>> and a haughty spirit before a fall.
> It is better to be of a lowly spirit with the poor
>> than to divide the spoil with the proud.
> Whoever gives thought to the word will discover good,
>> and blessed is he who trusts in the Lord.
> The wise of heart is called discerning,
>> and sweetness of speech increases persuasiveness.
> Good sense is a fountain of life to him who has it,
>> but the instruction of fools is folly.
> The heart of the wise makes his speech judicious
>> and adds persuasiveness to his lips.
> Gracious words are like a honeycomb,
>> sweetness to the soul and health to the body.
> There is a way that seems right to a man,
>> but its end is the way to death.

Pride is at the root of sin. Just as disobeying God is fundamentally the result of choosing our way over God's way, that rebellious mindset has its origin in pride. Pride is an infectious attitude of the heart out of which all our sinful choices flow. When we are prideful, our perspective is inwardly focused and self-serving. The first sin in the garden of Eden was birthed out of pride. Eve and Adam chose to eat of the forbidden fruit because the serpent seduced them with a lie that they would become wise like God. The Bible says in Genesis 3 that after the serpent lied, the fruit suddenly became desirable to Adam and Eve. Let's not also forget the Bible teaches that Satan was an angel in heaven before God cast him out for wanting to be God.

On one end of the pride spectrum is an aspirational pride that drives people on a quest for superiority. On the opposite end of the spectrum is self-loathing pride that rejects God's ascribed value to his creation. Everyone, regardless of one's position in life, must navigate the land mines of pride. Professional athletes, celebrities, CEOs, pastors, and, frankly, anyone in a position of authority or influence over others are especially vulnerable to being prideful. In fact, if you're bristling right now or offended by what you are reading, then that is an indicator pride is front and center in the blind spot of your life. When King Solomon writes in Proverbs 16 that pride goes before a fall (v. 18), he is describing an arrogant spirit that projects a false sense of security or invulnerability to weakness. He warns us that pride is the embodiment of trusting in ourselves to figure it all out and push through to get where we think we need to be.

But Jesus asks us to live differently. Knowing our predisposition is to be full of ourselves, he taught us to deny ourselves, take up our cross, and follow him. This jibes with Solomon's observation that while our ways may seem right to us (v. 25), they often are nothing more than a maze of dead ends. Consequently, we should not "follow our instincts" but instead prayerfully seek God in his Word and trust that his ways are infinitely better than our ways.

On the other end of the pride spectrum—180 degrees in the opposite direction of egomania—is a feeling of worthlessness. It may seem counterintuitive that thinking less of yourself is rooted in pride. But low self-esteem is often born out of a person's estimation of himself or herself apart from God's perspective. It's never good to allow anyone, including yourself, to define your self-worth by any measure other than God's standards. Satan wants nothing more than to render you useless to God. And one of his primary tactics is to frequently remind you of your past failures and painful experiences.

The words of others can cut deep and leave emotional and psychological wounds that last a lifetime. As Scripture says, "No human being can tame the tongue. It is a restless evil, full of deadly poison. With it we bless our Lord and Father, and with it we curse people who are made in the likeness of God. From the same mouth come blessing and cursing. My brothers, these things ought not to be so" (James 3:8–10).

To believe what anyone says about you more than what God says about you is to think more of them than God. You are a one-of-a-kind, limited-edition masterpiece. There is not another human being like you among the seven billion others on the planet. You're not just another face in the crowd; you were created on purpose with a purpose—to do good works that God planned for you before you were born (Ephesians 2:10). Like a priceless work of art, your value comes from your Creator. A painting of a green wheat field with a cypress tree might be just another painting, but add the artist's signature—Vincent van

114

Gogh—and suddenly the painting is a collector's piece. When God created you in his image, your stock rocketed to the heavens. *Who you are* is defined by *whose* you are.

And God wasn't satisfied with just being your creator. He also longed to be your heavenly Father. That's why he spared nothing—not even the life of his Son—to redeem you from being just a Social Security number to being a child of the One True King. As a professional baseball player, I was identified by the team I played with. The Mets, Dodgers, Giants, and Yankees adopted me into their organizations and paid a price to call me their own. But here's where the analogy breaks down: the contracts I signed with those teams had expiration dates. God's covenant, however, is a contract that never expires. As it says in Psalm 111:9, "He sent redemption to his people; *he has commanded his covenant forever.* Holy and awesome is his name!" (emphasis added). Your value to God never diminishes or fades. My baseball contracts were established on what I could do for the team. But God's covenant is established in his enabling, equipping, and empowering grace, mercy, and love.

In the very next verse, the psalmist adds that the "fear of the LORD is the beginning of wisdom." This is not some kind of cowering fear but instead a reverential fear based on awe and wonder. It's a recognition that God has the final say on who you are and ultimate veto power over dissenting opinions from anyone, anywhere, anytime. To dismiss or ignore this reality is to foolishly think you or someone else is wiser than God.

Genesis, the first book of the Bible, describes you and me

as God's image bearers: "God created man in his own image, in the image of God he created him; male and female he created them" (Genesis 1:27). As God's image bearers, we have a sense of morality, rationality, and spirituality unlike anything else God has created. As image bearers of God, we share his likeness in that we have a soul and spirit that will live for eternity. He created us this way so that we might have an intimate and personal relationship with him through his Son.

When professional athletes are enshrined into their respective Halls of Fame, a bronze bust of their likeness is usually created to honor their contributions to their sport. Yet the sculptors never seem to perfectly replicate the Hall of Famer's likeness. When Jesus died, however, he made a way for the sins that marred our image to be removed so that our likeness is just as God sees us—perfectly restored in him. As the apostle Paul describes in Colossians 3:10, we "have put on the new self, which is being renewed in knowledge after the image of its creator." Jesus's atoning sacrifice on the cross rescues, redeems, and restores us as God's image bearers, undefiled by a sinful and fallen world.

A HEART THAT EMBRACES HUMILITY

As we reflect God's heart, we understand our identity as God's masterpieces and image bearers of the Creator. We reject pride, even the pride of low self-esteem, because we know we've done nothing to earn God's favor. We embrace humility. In this, we follow the example of Jesus.

For Jesus to leave heaven and become like us, except without sin, is an amazing display of humility in and of itself. But that was just the beginning. While living among sinful human beings, he never took credit for his many great works, profound teaching, or mind-blowing miracles. When his supernatural wisdom and abilities were on display, Jesus always said he was simply obeying his Father—speaking words his Father gave him and doing the works his Father prepared for him to do. I believe humility is the most Christlike trait a person can possess. It's highly unlikely you will ever walk on water or heal the sick, but by God's grace, you can humbly serve and share the love of Christ without wanting recognition, credit, or applause.

As a professional athlete, I understand what it's like for fans and the media to idolize and worship me for my play on the field. But that fame and adoration is, frankly, vanity. To keep things in perspective, an athlete's records or feats are accomplished within the context of competing against other finite human beings who are limited by time, space, and gravity. Every athlete enjoys a limited window, maybe a few seasons, of peak performance before the wear and tear on the body is too much to overcome. Every time I stepped onto a ball field to showcase my talents, I was always one pitch, one step, one move, one turn, one swing, slide, or dive from stretching, tweaking, or breaking something in my body that could immediately render me useless to my team. Whether I knew it or not, I was completely dependent on the grace of God. That's equally true for my baseball career and life in general.

James 4:6 teaches us that God resists the proud but gives grace to the humble. I certainly have experienced that. As long as I thought I was in control, the more my life spiraled out of control. But when I asked God to rescue me from my drug and alcohol addiction, he was faithful to deliver on his promises. When I came to the end of myself in my pit of despair and cried out to God for healing, I realized the truth of God's promise in Matthew 6:33: "Seek first the kingdom of God and his righteousness, and all these things will be added to you."

THE BLESSED LIFE

Just as pride can potentially stain every thought, intent, motive, and action, humility can win the day every time if we follow Jesus's teaching in Matthew 5:3–12:

> Blessed are the poor in spirit, for theirs is the kingdom of heaven.
> Blessed are those who mourn, for they shall be comforted.
> Blessed are the meek, for they shall inherit the earth.
> Blessed are those who hunger and thirst for righteousness, for they shall be satisfied.
> Blessed are the merciful, for they shall receive mercy.
> Blessed are the pure in heart, for they shall see God.

Blessed are the peacemakers, for they shall be called sons of God.

Blessed are those who are persecuted for righteousness' sake, for theirs is the kingdom of heaven.

Blessed are you when others revile you and persecute you and utter all kinds of evil against you falsely on my account. Rejoice and be glad, for your reward is great in heaven, for so they persecuted the prophets who were before you.

It's been said that "attitude determines altitude." Cliché or not, the premise is that the perspective from which you see and interpret your circumstances has everything to do with how you respond in the midst of a situation. In this Scripture passage from the gospel of Matthew, Jesus identifies nine attitudes, or perspectives, that reflect God's heart.

Interestingly, Jesus tops his list with humility, although he doesn't identify it by name. "Poor in spirit" is the opposite of having a haughty spirit or prideful spirit. You would be hard pressed to associate the word *poor* in our modern vernacular with a positive or encouraging connotation. But to be "poor in spirit" actually means to be humble. How did I learn this? When God called me to be an itinerant evangelist more than ten years ago, one of the first things I did, in addition to diving into God's Word, was to begin reading everything I could find written by the late, world-renowned evangelist Billy Graham.

Here's an excerpt from his writings on what it means to be "poor in spirit":

We must be humble in our spirits. If you put the word "humble" in place of the word "poor," you will understand what He meant. In other words, when we come to God, we must realize our own sin and our spiritual emptiness and poverty. We must not be self-satisfied or proud in our hearts, thinking we don't really need God. If we are, God cannot bless us. The Bible says, "God opposes the proud but gives grace to the humble" (James 4:6). Pride can take all kinds of forms, but the worst is spiritual pride. Often the richer we are in things, the poorer we are in our hearts. Have you faced your own need of Christ? Do you realize that you are a sinner and need God's forgiveness? Don't let pride or anything else get in the way, but turn to Christ in humility and faith—and He will bless you and save you.[5]

When I was growing up on the tough streets of Los Angeles, crying was perceived as a sign of weakness—not an attribute you wanted to display in public. But Jesus said those who **mourn** will be blessed. Second Corinthians 7:10 states it this way: "Godly grief produces a repentance that leads to salvation without regret, whereas worldly grief produces death." I will never forget the godly sorrow I felt over my sin when I wept profusely as I received Jesus as my Savior. And when I sought my father's forgiveness for my bitterness toward him for abandoning me, the tears flowed as Jesus healed both our hearts.

As for being **meek**, you might think that sounds too much like being weak. Actually, meekness is a term that means strength under control. The best way I can illustrate this is with my baseball swing. When I swung my hardest, I usually had the worst results. My timing would be off, and I would usually swing under the baseball, resulting in a pop fly for an easy out. Other times when my swinging motion was exaggerated, I would fail to make contact at all. But when I eased up, not overdoing the power of my swing, the results were quite different. Though it looked almost effortless, when I made contact, the baseball soared out of the ballpark. Meekness is the attitude of trusting God to work out the details and accomplish his purpose in his perfect timing. The blessing, Jesus said, would be like an inheritance. You can't make an inheritance happen. You can only wait for an inheritance to come to fruition. Instead of you or me trying to make something happen in our own strength or ingenuity, God produces the results when we wait on him.

We can spend a lot of time and energy physically, financially, and emotionally trying to satisfy our **hunger and thirst** for the temporal things of this world. Experience has taught me that our insatiable appetites for stuff can't be satisfied. Human nature longs for bigger, better, newer, and shinier things. But God has promised us in his Word that the very thing that satisfies completely we can have in Christ Jesus. To hunger and thirst for righteousness is the desire to find one's contentment in knowing and doing the will of God. When we want what God desires for our lives, we will never hunger and thirst again for peace and purpose. Matthew 7:7–8 promises just as much: "Ask, and it will be given to you; seek, and you will find; knock, and it will be opened to you. For everyone who asks receives, and the one who seeks finds, and to the one who knocks it will be opened."

Playing Little League baseball, I learned my first lesson in being **merciful**. According to the rules of the game back then, if a team was ahead by ten runs or more by the fourth inning, the umpire could invoke the "mercy rule" and stop the game by declaring the team in the lead as the game's winner. In a lot of youth leagues today, the mercy rule can be applied if a team is leading by fifteen runs in the third inning. To be merciful is to show compassion or forgiveness to someone whom it is within one's power to punish. That's precisely what God did for sinners like you and me when he poured out his wrath on his Son, thereby sparing us the punishment we deserve. Since we have been shown mercy by God, how much more should we be willing to show mercy to others? Whom do you know who needs to experience your compassion and forgiveness? By paying it forward, you just might help someone understand their desperate need for God's mercy as well.

When Jesus declared, "Blessed are the **pure in heart**," (emphasis added) he was emphasizing the importance of a person's inward condition over their outward appearance. The Jewish religious leaders of Jesus's day did not impress or deceive him. They could recite the more than six hundred laws of Judaism verbatim. They knew the letter of the law but didn't understand the spirit of the law. The Pharisees knew legalism but didn't understand God's grace. And Jesus called them out for their haughty and prideful spirits in Matthew 23:25–26: "Woe to you, scribes and Pharisees, hypocrites! For you clean the outside of the cup and the plate, but inside they are full of greed and self-indulgence. You blind Pharisee! First clean the inside of the cup and the plate, that the outside also may be clean."

As a professional athlete, I was in great shape physically, but on the inside, I was a broken mess. That's sort of the same situation that Jesus saw in the Pharisees, who seemed like perfect law keepers on the outside but whose inner selves were far from God. The fact is, God's laws can't save you or me from our sins, but they do show us that we need saving. The "pure in heart" Jesus commended aren't motivated by a list of dos and don'ts but a desire to worship God in spirit and truth. They experience God's presence in their lives because they've committed themselves wholeheartedly to the process of knowing him and being known by him. They guard their hearts in Christ Jesus because they know what their hearts are capable of producing. Jesus warned in Matthew 15:19, "Out of the heart come evil thoughts, murder, adultery, sexual immorality, theft, false witness, slander." That's why Jesus came to seek and save the lost, so that all those who are spiritually blinded to their need for God might understand the deceptiveness of their hearts and turn to God in true repentance. When we come to Christ by faith, he replaces our heart with his heart so we increasingly desire the things of God. The pure in heart don't take their cues from society, public opinion surveys, or what's trending on social media. Aware of God's holiness and perfection, the pure in heart understand that who they are in private, when no one else is looking, is a true measure of their devotion to God.

Jesus called his followers to be **peacemakers**. Notice he didn't say peace*keepers*. Peacekeepers go along to get along. Peacemakers are ambassadors of reconciliation. Peacekeepers maintain the status quo. Peacemakers step into the middle of situations that aren't peaceful and show others how to love their enemies. Peacekeepers act like thermometers, simply reading the current conditions. Peacemakers act like thermostats, which set the temperature. In Matthew 5:43–47 (NKJV), Jesus provided the prescription for how to be a peacemaker:

> You have heard that it was said, "You shall love your neighbor and hate your enemy." But I say to you, love your enemies, bless those who curse you, do good to those who hate you, and pray for those who spitefully use you and persecute you, that you may be sons of your Father in heaven; for He makes His sun rise on the evil and on the good, and sends rain on the just and on the unjust. For if you love those who love you, what reward have you? Do not even the tax collectors do the same? And if you greet your brethren only, what do you do more *than others*? Do not even the tax collectors do so?

It's only when we love the unlovely and forgive those difficult people in our lives that the light of God's love can shine in the darkness. By God's grace, I've had to learn the truth of the biblical virtue to love and pray for those who exploit others for personal gain. Over the course of my career, I've had unscru-pulous business partners betray my trust and good faith. Their deceptively selfish decisions caused me great hardship and seasons of financial instability. I have since forgiven those who conspired against me. Furthermore, I pray that they experience God's grace, mercy, and forgiveness through a personal relationship with Jesus. Instead of being bitter and vengeful about what was stolen from me, I choose to trust in God's continued faithfulness to meet my every need. My enemies can rob me of financial resources, but they can't rob me of my joy in the Lord. There's something liberating about transferring ownership of all that I have to God. Now I no longer bear the sense of loss and injustice that once haunted me. What I have and what I lost is God's to do with as he chooses. When you are sold out to the One who gave it all, everything you have is his.

A HEART TO SAVE OTHERS

One of the most important ways, if not the most important way, to reflect God's heart is to help people understand their need to turn to him for the forgiveness of their sins. The COVID-19 global pandemic has reminded everyone how fragile life is. The threshold between life and death is as invisible as the coronavirus. In light of eternity, life is like a vapor. You can be here today and gone tomorrow. Hebrews 9:27 states that everyone has an appointment with death. And those who don't profess Christ as

Savior in this life must face God's judgment in the next life for all eternity.

What a tragedy it would be if one of your family members, friends, neighbors, or coworkers passed away to a Christless eternity without your sharing your story with them—how you were a starving beggar before you received the Bread of Life. What is preventing you from sharing the best news ever with those who need to receive Jesus's gift of forgiveness and salvation? Are you fearful they might ridicule or reject you? Jesus was ridiculed and rejected for you and me. Do you love those who need to know about Jesus's love? The Bible says the best way you can love someone is by telling them how much God loves them: "In this the love of God was made manifest among us, that God sent his only Son into the world, so that we might live through him. In this is love, not that we have loved God but that he loved us and sent his Son to be the propitiation for our sins. Beloved, if God so loved us, we also ought to love one another" (1 John 4:9–11).

Propitiation means payment. Jesus, who was sinless, took our sin upon himself on the cross to pay the death penalty we deserved. When we share that eternal truth with others, we are truly loving one another. Conversely, to not share that God is love and Jesus is the way, the truth, and the life is to not love one another.

You might be familiar with illusionist and comedian Penn Jillette, who tours the world as part of the amazingly talented and successful Penn and Teller magician duo. You're likely not surprised to know that Penn, as an avowed atheist, doesn't respect some Christians. But you might be surprised by his reasoning. In a video blog Penn posted a few years ago, he recounts an incident where after one of his shows, a man politely gave him a Gideon New Testament Bible.

"I've always said, I don't respect people who don't proselytize," Penn remarked. "I don't respect that at all. If you believe in a heaven and a hell, and people could be going to hell or not getting eternal life or whatever, and you think it's not really worth telling them this because it would make it socially awkward. How much do you have to hate somebody to not proselytize? How much do you have to hate someone to believe everlasting life is possible and not tell them that?" To further make his point, Penn said, "If I believed, beyond a shadow of a doubt, that a truck was coming at you, and you didn't believe it, that that truck was bearing down on you, there's a certain point that I tackle you, and this is more important than that. This guy was a really good guy. He was polite, honest, and sane, and he cared enough about me to proselytize and give me a Bible."[6]

How convicting is that rationale about the importance of sharing your faith in Christ from, of all people, someone who doesn't believe God exists? If you are hesitant to share the gospel or apathetic about where someone will spend eternity, that may indicate you love this world more than you love God. We're warned in 1 John 2:15–17, "Do not love the world or the things in the world. If anyone loves the world, the love of the Father is not in him. For all that is in the world—the desires of the flesh and the desires of the eyes and pride of life—is not from the Father but is from the world. And the world is passing away along with its desires, but whoever does the will of God abides forever."

It's easy to be distracted by the things of this world. With our social media, music, movies, collegiate and professional sports, video games, politics, hobbies, travel, and recreational activities, we can get busy and entertain ourselves into oblivion. But ask yourself, Do my personal interests have a shelf life beyond this world? Yet when we engage in the mission of God, those priorities make a difference that can change lives forever.

THINK ABOUT IT

1. What does it mean that Christians are part of a "royal priesthood"?
2. In what ways are you "set apart" for God?
3. How is the church like the human body?
4. Is your faith being tested currently? If so, how?
5. What does it mean to have a biblical worldview?
6. Do you struggle with pride, low self-esteem, or both? What are the results of that in your life?
7. What does it mean to be created in God's image?
8. Of the nine "blessed" characteristics in Matthew 5, which of them do you demonstrate in your life? Which ones don't describe you at all?

RECLAIM GOD'S BEST

His divine power has granted to us all things
that pertain to life and godliness, through the
knowledge of him who called us to his own glory
and excellence, by which he has granted to us
his precious and very great promises, so that
through them you may become partakers of the
divine nature, having escaped from the corruption
that is in the world because of sinful desire.

2 PETER 1:3–4

Since their first season in 1962, the New York Mets have claimed two World Series titles—in 1969 and 1986. Both championships were won under the most unlikely of circumstances, which has garnered the Metropolitans two well-deserved nicknames——"Amazin' Mets" and "Miracle Mets." Actually, the first moniker was made in jest by the team's founding manager, former Yankees skipper Casey Stengel, who came out of retirement at age seventy-two to coach the start-up franchise made up largely of has-been and want-to-be professional baseball players. If you think that description is too harsh, consider their first season record of 40 wins and 120 losses. "Come see my Amazin' Mets," Casey Stengel once said. "I've been in this game a hundred years, but I see new ways to lose I never knew existed before."[1] The Mets lost at least 109 games in each of their first four seasons. During their first seven seasons, the Mets lost a total of 737 games and never finished higher than ninth place in the ten-team National League.

But then something happened in 1969. The same year American astronaut Neil Armstrong walked on the moon and Woodstock gave birth to the sexual revolution, the "Miracle Mets" won one hundred regular-season games, including thirty-eight of their last forty-nine contests. In an era mired in the Vietnam War, race riots, and the assassinations of Bobby Kennedy and Martin Luther King Jr., America was a nation gripped in fear and hate. It's hard to believe, in light of today's divisive culture, that not too long ago it seemed even worse. If ever America needed to be united, the Mets were the answer for that time. They swept the Atlanta Braves to win the National League pennant and dominated the mighty Baltimore Orioles, winners of 109 games. After losing game one to the Orioles, the Mets won the next four games, including game five before the home crowd in Shea Stadium. The underdog of underdogs had symbolically brought hope and healing to a country in turmoil. The 1969 Miracle Mets taught America to believe that what might seem inconceivable could be more than improbable and even possible, if not incredible. And although the Mets haven't won another World Series title since our last parade in 1986, hope springs eternal every spring training that this just might be the year for another miracle.

As World Series champions come and go with the passing of one season to the next, the Bible promises that God's divine power equips Christians to reclaim God's best in a world corrupt with sin. Meanwhile, our materialistic culture bombards us with a twenty-first-century spin on the same messaging with which the serpent deceived Adam and Eve in the garden. Advertisers tell us we need this, that, or the other thing to be happy and successful. Marketing companies pull our heart strings in an effort to subtly shame or guilt us into thinking we would be irresponsible to deny the "very best" for those we love. Furthermore, our culture glorifies this mindset with a virtuous label called the American Dream—an ambition or goal to be whoever you want to be and do whatever you want to do, so long as you don't hurt or infringe on the rights of anyone else in the process. Yet the reality that often follows the vain pursuit of self-satisfaction is the painful cost of hurting others. I've already described the painful consequences that divorce and addiction cost me and my family as a result of my vain and selfish pursuits of my ways over God's ways.

GETTING AN EDGE

As we continue to think through what it means to reclaim God's best for our lives—the seventh spiritual RBI (realities beyond imagination)—I'm reminded that in the world of athletic competition, the name of the game at every level, and in every sport, is to discover and leverage whatever competitive advantage is available within the rules of competition. On a foundational level, in both individual and team competition, the person or team who physically trains the most usually has a competitive advantage in strength, speed, and endurance. On a tactical level, the person or team who knows their opponent's weaknesses the best can often exploit those vulnerabilities for a competitive advantage. On an emotional and psychological level, teams and individuals who are the most determined, hopeful, and optimistic usually possess a relentless drive to succeed that outlasts their opponents. Unfortunately for some individuals and teams, the lure to be the best draws them beyond the boundaries of their sport to pursue an illegal competitive advantage through the use of performance-enhancing drugs. As with Adam and Eve's lust for the forbidden fruit in the garden of Eden, athletes can sometimes succumb to the narcissistic temptation to be the best at any cost. Frankly, that's why collegiate, professional, and Olympic sports federations perform random drug testing of their athletes as a deterrent to cheating the sport and its fans of the integrity of the game.

Major League Baseball bears its own blight for players

who have used performance-enhancing drugs. Steroids have been banned in MLB since 1991. However, the league did not implement league-wide performance-enhancing-drug testing until 2003. To their credit, some baseball greats from this era have regretfully admitted to using steroids during their careers. But a cloud of suspicion continues to hang over the careers of others.

The problem with performance-enhancing drugs in sports is a symptom of a spiritual issue, the drive to win at all costs. But it also has a positive parallel in the transforming work that God does in the life of a Christ follower. When someone surrenders their heart to the Creator, he gives them everything they need to thrive and succeed in the life he purposed them to live. You might even call it God's performance-enhancing power. Do you think that's a stretch? Consider the words of 2 Peter 1:3–8:

His divine power has granted to us all things that pertain to life and godliness, through the knowledge of him who called us to his own glory and excellence, by which he has granted to us his precious and very great promises, so that through them you may become partakers of the divine nature, having escaped from the corruption that is in the world because of sinful desire. For this very reason, make every effort to supplement your faith with virtue, and virtue with knowledge, and knowledge with self-control, and self-control with steadfastness, and steadfastness with godliness, and godliness with brotherly affection, and brotherly affection with love.

For if these qualities are yours and are increasing, they keep you from being ineffective or unfruitful in the knowledge of our Lord Jesus Christ.

Please don't miss the application of this biblical passage in your life. To call it a game changer could be an understatement when you consider its implications for experiencing the best life for which God created you.

The first reality to acknowledge in this passage is that when God rescues you from "the corruption that is in the world because of your sinful desire," he sets you free from the bondage of sin. Instead of being a slave to your sinful desires, you "become partakers of the divine nature." This happens because God "has granted to us his precious and very great promises."

Consequently, when God adopts you into his family, you don't have to wait until you die to experience the promise of eternal life. According to this passage, God's "divine power has granted to us all things that pertain to life and godliness, through the knowledge of him who called us to his own glory and excellence." This means that when God transforms you from the inside out, he also enables you to live excellently for his glory while you are here on earth. To do so is effectively to praise him for saving you from your sins by displaying his wonder-working power in your life. When people see how you live for Christ, and not just for yourself, your obedience and faithfulness to his Word glorify God.

And by the promise of God's power in your life, he will

add the following faith-enhancing attributes: virtue, knowledge, self-control, steadfastness, godliness, brotherly affection, and love. So let's take a few minutes to unpack these faith-building, Jesus-loving, God-honoring characteristics.

QUALITIES OF A QUALITY LIFE

Virtue is defined as behavior showing high moral standards. But this Scripture passage isn't about conceding to society's version of morality. The world teaches that morality is subjective, based on an individual's definition of truth. But God defines morality based on his universal standard of truth found in the Ten Commandments (Exodus 20:1–17). Here is my contemporary translation of God's list of moral requirements: *Don't worship other gods. Don't idolize things or people. Only use the Lord's name for honor and praise. Set aside one day of the week as sacred for drawing close to God. Honor your father and your mother. Don't murder, commit adultery, steal, lie, or covet.*

By the world's moral standards, God's commandments are mere suggestions. The culture's thinking goes something like this: You are your own god. Idol worship is simply pursuing your passion above everything else. Taking the Lord's name in vain will earn you an Emmy or Oscar nomination. Sundays are "Miller Time" or time for any other alcoholic beverage you desire to drink—responsibly, of course. Parents are depicted as buffoons in television sitcoms. Murder is a choice. Adultery is an affair. Stealing is defaulting on a loan. Lying is misleading, misspeaking, or misremembering. And coveting is aspiring to be like someone else.

Don't be deceived; what the culture describes as good doesn't come close to God's standards of virtue. Jesus said as much when he encountered a young man who thought he knew what was good and virtuous, as reported in Matthew 19:16–17 (NKJV): "Now behold, one came and said to Him, 'Good Teacher, what good thing shall I do that I may have eternal life?' So He said to him, 'Why do you call Me good? No one *is* good but One, *that is*, God. But if you want to enter into life, keep the commandments.'"

You see, God is the very definition of all that is good. And his Word promises that he has given those who love him everything they need in Jesus Christ and the power of the Holy Spirit to live morally, ethically, and sexually pure lives as a testimony of praise to the "Father of lights, with whom there is no variation or shadow due to change" (James 1:17).

And to virtue add **knowledge**, the Scripture continues. *Knowledge* is defined as facts, information, and skills acquired by a person through experience or education. The most fruitful form of knowledge is that which is transferred from the theoretical to the practical, from conceptual to the concrete, from possible to doable to done. Experience is often the best teacher.

Your faith remains weak unless it's exercised. When we exercise our muscles, they become stronger; the same is true of your faith. Faith is believing that where God guides, he provides;

where God directs, he protects; and where God leads, he feeds. Whether it's walking by faith and not sight or waiting by faith even when what we want is in sight, to know God more is to experience more of him in our lives. And to experience him more in our lives requires that we do the things that require more of him in our lives, such as loving unconditionally, forgiving exponentially, and serving intentionally. It's been said that religion is spelled D-O—as in special works to earn God's favor. Christianity, on the other hand, is spelled D-O-N-E—as in Christ's finished work on the cross to make sinful human beings right with God. Consequently, Christians don't do works of faith to be saved. We do faithful works *because* we are saved.

> **Your faith remains weak unless it's exercised. When we exercise our muscles, they become stronger; the same is true of your faith.**

And to knowledge add **self-control**. Proverbs 24:5 says, "A wise man is full of strength, and a man of knowledge enhances his might." Self-control is the fruit of the Spirit in a Christian's life that disciplines one's thoughts, speech, and actions for greater impact. For example, it's one thing to know what to say, but equally if not more important is to know when and how to say it. This couldn't be truer than when it comes to sharing or explaining the gospel. Just because I know Jesus is "the way, and the truth, and the life" doesn't mean someone else is ignorant for not knowing or believing the same. It's been said that people don't care how much you know until they know how much you care. Often before someone hears the gospel from us, they need to see it in us. When our words follow our actions, what we say is more believable. We find an expression of this in 1 Peter 3:15–16: "In your hearts honor Christ the Lord as holy, always being prepared to make a defense to anyone who asks you for a reason for the hope that is in you; yet do it with gentleness and respect, having a good conscience, so that, when you are slandered, those who revile your good behavior in Christ may be put to shame."

When self-discipline is added to knowledge, words aren't wasted, opportunities aren't squandered; life is lived with purpose and an intentionality focused on being ready to point people to Jesus. The Bible says just as a thousand-pound horse is guided by a small bit in its mouth and a huge ship is directed by an inconspicuous rudder underneath the vessel, the tongue—for better or worse—controls the body. "So also the tongue is a small member, yet it boasts of great things. How great a forest is set ablaze by such a small fire! And the tongue is a fire, a world of unrighteousness. The tongue is set among our members, staining the whole body, setting on fire the entire course of life, and set on fire by hell" (James 3:5–6).

Words matter. They have consequences. And when you post them on social media platforms, they can follow you for the rest of your life. So choose your words wisely. Make them count for eternity. And the next time you feel the need to be right or win an argument, ask yourself what's more important—being right or being in a right relationship? Don't forget, whatever someone else might say or do, Christians have already been made right with God—justified in his sight by the forgiveness of their sin through the death, burial, and resurrection of his Son. Christ followers aren't called to win debates or arguments. The Bible says in Romans 1:16, "I am not ashamed of the gospel, for it is the power of God for salvation to everyone who believes." As an evangelist, I have the privilege of sharing the life-changing message of the gospel. My responsibility is simply to be faithful in sharing the hope I have in Jesus. God is responsible for drawing the harvest of believers. That is why Jesus said in the gospels to pray to the Lord of the harvest.

And to self-control add **steadfastness**. Steadfast means to be loyal, faithful, committed, devoted, dedicated, dependable, unchanging, reliable, unyielding, unwavering, uncompromising, relentless, determined, single-minded, unhesitating, and true. These are the qualities that make for an excellent teammate. What's ironic about some of those who succumbed to the temptation to use performance-enhancing drugs is that they likely would have had Hall of Fame careers had they simply remained committed to strengthening their bodies the right way, honing their skills, and making the necessary sacrifices to be the best they could be. But because of a lack of self-control, their egos got the best of them.

More importantly, the characteristic of steadfastness embodies what it means to be sold out to the cause of Christ. The only way Christians can live in this world but yet not be of the world is to be steadfast in their faith. When doubts, questions, and temptations come—and they will—steadfastness keeps us running the race of faith with our eyes on the prize of the "upward call of

God" in Jesus Christ. In Philippians 3, the apostle Paul says this is how mature Christians think.

People change. Culture changes. Public opinion is finicky. Laws change. Leaders come and go. Seasons change. But God's Word never changes. It is truth for all people, for all time. That's why Christians are called to remain faithful to God's Word even when some who call themselves Christians are unfaithful to its teachings. If you have yielded to the culture's influence and compromised the authority of Scripture, please repent for wavering, and recommit yourself to being single-minded in your devotion to obeying the Word of God.

And to steadfastness, add **godliness**. Godliness is the characteristic of living in faithful obedience to God. Have you ever heard of someone described as a godly man or woman? If so, you probably know that person's reputation as one who devoutly and wholeheartedly applies the precepts of God's Word to their daily life. What they talk about and how they spend their time and money reflect an all-consuming focus on living for God and not themselves. In 1 Timothy 6:6–10, Paul writes to his protégé in the ministry: "Godliness with contentment is great gain, for we brought nothing into the world, and we cannot take anything out of the world. But if we have food and clothing, with these we will be content. But those who desire to be rich fall into temptation, into a snare, into many senseless and harmful desires that plunge people into ruin and destruction. For the love of money is a root of all kinds of evils. It is through this craving that some have wandered away from the faith and pierced themselves with many pangs."

Paul warns Timothy in this passage that one of the greatest threats to godliness is the "love of money." An insatiable craving for the things of this world has robbed many people of the eternal riches found only in a thriving relationship with Jesus. I can speak from experience and tell you that there were seasons in my life when I had a lot more money and material possessions than I have now, but my contentment meter was in the deficit. Contentment is a hallmark of godliness. If all you had was food, clothing, and shelter, could you be content? Would your relationship with Jesus not only suffice but supersede your circumstances? Contentment is the crown jewel in life. Unfortunately, our society's economic engine is largely driven by consumers' looking for contentment in all the wrong ways. A daily pursuit of the latest and greatest, biggest and best, and newest and shiniest has many Christians maintaining lifestyles that leave little margin—much less mission—for the things of God. In answering which is God's greatest commandment among the religious laws of his day, Jesus replied in Matthew 22:37–38, "You shall love the Lord your God with all your heart and with all your soul and with all your mind. This is the great and first commandment." Now, that is the epitome of godliness.

And to godliness add **brotherly affection**. Championship teams usually share this one characteristic, though it's generally called by a different name—chemistry. This is an emotional bond founded on a unified purpose and built on mutual respect. It's the type of affection commonly found in a family, a bond that is unbreakable by outside forces. Brotherly affection is synonymous with "all for one and one for all." I experienced this comradery with my World Series championship teams as a Met and Yankee. Teams that are successful stick together in good times and bad. They don't hold grudges or keep score of personal offenses against each other. Instead, they encourage one another and always believe the best in each other. When it comes to being on God's team, brotherly affection is essential for showing and sharing the love of Christ. If brothers and sisters in Christ don't have one another's backs and aren't quick to forgive one another, then why would those lost without a saving faith in Jesus care to consider the implications of the gospel for their lives?

A daily pursuit of the latest and greatest, biggest and best, and newest and shiniest has many Christians maintaining lifestyles that leave little margin—much less mission—for the things of God.

And add to brotherly affection **love**. The last in this list of promises of God-enhancing power from 2 Peter is God's love. In 1 John 3:16 this is described as a supernatural, sacrificial form of love: "By this we know love, that he laid down his life for us, and we ought to lay down our lives for the brothers." Jesus displayed the ultimate expression of love when he sacrificed his life on our behalf so that we could be made right with God. Furthermore, Jesus said it directly in John 15:12–14: "This is my commandment, that you love one another as I have loved you. Greater love has no one than this, that someone lay down his life for his friends. You are my friends if you do what I command you."

Jesus said we are his friends if we are willing to deny ourselves—fill in the blank—whatever might be required of us so that someone else would see Jesus in us and experience the love of God as a result of our sacrifice. Jesus explained further in Mark 12 that second only to loving him with all our heart, soul, mind, and strength, we should love our neighbor like ourselves. The application of this command is that just as we wouldn't deny ourselves anything to sustain our lives, likewise we should not deny our neighbors anything to sustain their lives. In a spiritual sense, this means that once an individual receives the lifesaving, life-changing gift of forgiveness in Jesus Christ, they should be willing to spare no personal sacrifice to show and share the same life-transforming message of the gospel with anyone who stands condemned in their sins.

In 1 Corinthians 13:4–8, the apostle Paul teaches us what godly love is and isn't in plain and certain terms: "Love is patient and kind; love does not envy or boast; it is not arrogant or rude. It does not insist on its own way; it is not irritable or resentful; it does not rejoice at wrongdoing, but rejoices with the truth. Love bears all things, believes all things, hopes all things, endures all things. Love never ends. As for prophecies, they will pass away; as for tongues, they will cease; as for knowledge, it will pass away."

While this is a popular Bible reading at wedding ceremonies and certainly is the prescription for a thriving and healthy marriage, the transforming truths of this passage are equally applicable for every God-honoring relationship.

Unlike the long-term negative effects of metabolic steroids, the faith-enhancing attributes we have just unpacked have no unpleasant side effects. Instead, they promise just the opposite—a life that is fruitful, effective, and growing in the knowledge of our Lord Jesus Christ.

THE RIGHT TO LIFE

Possibly the gravest deception our society has bought from the Father of Lies, Satan himself, is that our personal rights, freedoms, and liberties as Americans supersede God's divine ownership and authority over our lives. Thomas Jefferson wrote in our cherished Declaration of Independence: "We hold these truths to be self-evident, that all men are created equal, that they are endowed by their Creator with certain unalienable Rights, that among these are Life, Liberty, and the pursuit of Happiness." Jefferson couldn't have been more correct or intentional to have employed the precise verbiage and organized it in such a way as to communicate the heart of democracy in this profoundly American virtue.

First, please notice that Americans, and for that matter all human beings on the face of the earth, are given their rights by their Creator. These rights aren't awarded to the highest bidder. They can't be earned and aren't merit based. As an endowment from our Creator, these rights are by definition an inheritance from God Almighty.

Second, Jefferson describes these rights as inherently undeniable by calling them "unalienable rights." *Unalienable* means "not transferable to another or not capable of being taken away or denied."[2]

Third, these rights are highlighted and ordered specifically in sequence as "Life, Liberty and the pursuit of Happiness." In Jefferson's systematic order, one right is a prerequisite for the next. In other words, to realize liberty, you must first have life, and to realize your pursuit of happiness, you might first enjoy liberty. Such linear thinking should lead us to the logical conclusion that all our rights flow from the right to life.

So if our country was founded on this virtue, then why on earth does the United States of America rank seventh in abortion rates out of 193 member provinces of the United Nations? According to the United Nations 2020 World Abortion Policies report, 19.6 abortions occur annually in the United States for every 1,000 women ages 15 to 44.[3] When you apply that abortion rate across the US population demographic, the exponential effect of killing life in a mother's womb numbers in the hundreds of thousands every year in America. There have been more than 62 million abortion deaths since the US Supreme Court legalized abortion in 1973.[4] Intellectual honesty demands we acknowledge that the pro-choice movement being advanced in our culture under the guise of "reproductive rights" is incompatible with our Declaration of Independence that secures every human being the right to life. As an "unalienable right," the right to life should be protected at every stage and phase of life from the womb to the tomb. Yet abortion is the unmistakable act of human beings choosing to deny the right to life of other human beings in the womb, which is precisely what happens when a human life is forcibly and prematurely ended at any point after conception and before birth.

And just think, a pro-life argument founded on the Declaration of Independence alone pales in comparison to the biblical ethic for life. The Old Testament prophet Isaiah boldly describes the utter foolishness, pride, and arrogance of human beings to think and act as though they are God, who creates and sustains life. Isaiah 29:15–16 reads,

> Ah, you who hide deep from the LORD your counsel,
>> whose deeds are in the dark,
>> and who say, "Who sees us? Who knows us?"
> You turn things upside down!
> Shall the potter be regarded as the clay,
> that the thing made should say of its maker,
>> "He did not make me";
> or the thing formed say of him who formed it,
>> "He has no understanding"?

Clearly, Isaiah is making the point that God is the potter and human beings are the clay—subject to his hands. Earlier in this book, we explored the psalmist's description of how God's eyes are on us constantly while we are being knit together, or under construction, in our mother's womb. When King David declares further in the Psalms that human beings are fearfully and wonderfully made, he is ascribing reverential awe for those created in his image. Fashioned with a soul that will live forever, human beings are distinguished as the masterpieces of God's created order. As the potter, God is the initiator and giver of every good and perfect gift in our lives, according to James 1:17. In addition to being our Creator, God is also our Master and Judge. This is why the prophet declares in Isaiah 64:7–9,

> There is no one who calls upon your name,
> > who rouses himself to take hold of you;
> for you have hidden your face from us,
> > and have made us melt in the hand of our iniquities.

> But now, O Lord, you are our Father;
> > we are the clay, and you are our potter;
> > we are all the work of your hand.
> Be not so terribly angry, O Lord,
> > and remember not iniquity forever.
> > Behold, please look, we are all your people.

Just like Isaiah's pleas for mercy from a righteous and holy God, we would do well to cry out to God for grace and mercy in repentance for the sins of our nation. The blood and carnage inflicted upon America by an abortion industry intent on playing God and preying on the most vulnerable of his creation is a blight on society that can be removed only by the innocent, sinless blood of Jesus Christ. And God stands eagerly ready and willing to forgive abortion providers, those who have had abortions, as well as those who have remained indifferent to the sanctity of human life. Claim God's promise in 2 Peter 3:9: "The Lord is not slow to fulfill his promise as some count slowness, but is patient toward you, not wishing that any should perish, but that all should reach repentance."

THINK ABOUT IT

1. In what ways have you been tempted to win at any cost?
2. How has God's power shown up in your life?
3. Looking at the qualities listed in 2 Peter 1:5–7, how would you define virtue?
4. How would you define knowledge?
5. How important is self-control?
6. What does steadfastness look like in your life?
7. Do you know anyone who seems to embody the biblical definition of goodness?
8. How is brotherly affection like team spirit?
9. How is the Bible's definition of love different from the world's definition?

RESTORE GOD'S PEACE

I know the plans I have for you, declares the
LORD, plans for welfare and not for evil, to
give you a future and a hope. Then you will
call upon me and come and pray to me, and I
will hear you. You will seek me and find me,
when you seek me with all your heart.

JEREMIAH 29:11–13

One of the few things I miss from my baseball career is suiting up in my uniform and taking the field with my teammates. Something about wearing the team logo and colors never got old. The uniforms were made of the highest quality materials and designed for flexibility. The fabrics were water resistant and breathed to help keep you cool on hot summer days. And in those chilly games in early spring and late fall, the uniforms had a lining to trap the warmth. The baseball helmets fit your head like a glove and provided a sense of security against those hundred-mile-per-hour darts coming at you from sixty-and-a-half feet away. Wearing a uniform with my last name across my back made me feel like I belonged. I had made it to the top of my profession. Along with my teammates, there was no opposing baseball stadium that we didn't think we could conquer.

But I put on a different uniform now. It's called the full armor of God. This uniform is required to defend against and defeat the daily stealth attacks from the Enemy. Sadly, too many Christians think this uniform is optional. But choosing not to put on God's armor is conceding defeat and cheating yourself out of personally experiencing the promises of God's powerful presence.

It would be like dismissing Major League Baseball's published findings in 2020 that the 2017 World Series champion Houston Astros cheated in the Fall Classic against the Los Angeles Dodgers. The nine-page commissioner's report[1] explains at great length how the Astros stole catchers' signs throughout the 2017 season by picking them up on a video feed and then letting the batters know what types of pitches were coming. The investigation's findings were also confirmed by former Astros pitcher Mike Fiers, who admitted as much to the *Athletic*, a sports journalism website.[2] The commissioner's report notes further that former Dodgers player Alex Cora, who was then an Astros coach, coordinated the cheating scheme when he "arranged for a video-room technician to install a monitor displaying the center-field camera feed immediately outside of the Astros dugout."[3]

With this equipment in place, Astros players could readily view the opposing catcher's signs in real time, decipher them, then transfer the information to batters by banging a trash can with a bat to signal specifically whether the pitcher was about to offer up a fastball, curveball, slider, cutter, or any other variety. Knowing what we know now about the Astros' illegal scheme, even the most jaded skeptics and Dodger-haters are left to wonder if the technology-driven heist of the Dodger's pitching signs robbed the city of Los Angeles of its first World Series championship since 1988.

Personally, I think it's a foregone conclusion that Astros batters knew what type of pitches were coming their way. They weren't clairvoyant. They didn't accidently or miraculously decode the signals. Coaches, players, and team staff conspired to devise a scheme to give their batters a competitive advantage on Major League Baseball's biggest stage when the stakes were highest. And so the World Series was like batting practice as Houston hitters piled up eighteen runs on twenty-six hits and six home runs in two series-changing victories over Dodger pitchers Yu Darvish, Clayton Kershaw, and Brandon Morrow, who had all previously dominated their postseason opponents.

OUR ENEMY

You and I also have an enemy trying to steal victory from us. The Bible is clear about the Enemy's strategy to divide and conquer the body of Christ through deceitful schemes. He espouses counterfeit truths grounded in faulty premises. He disguises utter foolishness as wisdom. He distracts with the lure of entertainment, lust, ambition, and greed. He promotes vanity as if it were a virtue. He employs false teachers and fake Christians—wolves in sheep's clothing—to pervert the gospel and mislead masses of people about the true meaning of love and godliness. He uses religion to replace the only thing that can truly heal a person's heart—a relationship with Jesus. He elevates all forms of spirituality to try to appease the need every person has to know God. In 1 Peter 5:8–9 (NKJV) we find a stark warning that would be foolish to take lightly: "Be sober, be vigilant; because your adversary the devil walks about like a roaring lion, seeking whom he may devour. Resist him, steadfast in the faith, knowing that the same sufferings are experienced by your brotherhood in the world."

Some Bible translations refer to "self-control" and being "watchful"—"always on the lookout"—for the enemy's schemes and attacks. If you have ever read *National Geographic* or watched the Animal Planet channel, you've probably learned that a lion stalks stealthily toward its prey only to pounce when the victim is least aware and most vulnerable. The king of the jungle doesn't make a grand announcement of his intentions to subdue his prey by biting and breaking their neck before ripping them apart limb by limb. No, a lion cleverly and quietly conceals himself in the tall grass or behind a rock, tree, or cluster of vegetation before pouncing on its unassuming victim. It's not until the damage has been done, the prey conquered, that the lion roars in elation over his conquest.

We are warned in Scripture about this lionlike adversary. To heed this warning, we must first acknowledge that there is an enemy who is intent on destroying both our lives and our witness for Christ. After recognizing the reality of spiritual warfare in our lives, we are called to actively resist the Enemy. Surely you've heard the old adage that if you fail to plan, you plan to fail. That couldn't be truer. You can plan on this: our Enemy is cunningly planning to trick, cheat, deceive, defraud, double-cross, and bamboozle us.

Our enemy is cunningly planning to trick, cheat, deceive, defraud, double-cross, and bamboozle us.

God's Word instructs us to remain steadfast in the faith. Steadfast means dutiful, resolute, firm, and unwavering. How do we do that? With the full armor of God, as the apostle Paul describes in Ephesians 6: 13–18:

> Therefore take up the whole armor of God, that you may be able to withstand in the evil day, and having done all, to stand firm. Stand therefore, having fastened on the belt of truth, and having put on the breastplate of righteousness, and, as shoes for your feet, having put on the readiness given by the gospel of peace. In all circumstances take up the shield of faith, with which you can extinguish all the flaming darts of the evil one; and take the helmet of salvation, and the sword of the Spirit, which is the word of God, praying at all times in the Spirit,

with all prayer and supplication. To that end, keep alert with all perseverance, making supplication for all the saints.

OUR ARMOR

Paul identifies the **belt of truth** as the first essential piece of our godly uniform to resist the Enemy—also known as "the father of lies" (John 8:44). Jesus said in John 14:6, "I am the way, and the truth, and the life. No one comes unto the Father except through me." It is only by the truth of God's perfect Word in Scripture that we can discern fact from fiction. God's Word holds everything together in perfect harmony.

The full counsel of Scripture leaves no stone unturned when it comes to navigating the land mines, quicksand, hanging cliffs, wrong turns, and dead ends on this earthly journey. God's Word, our belt of truth, instructs us that wide is the path of destruction, but narrow is the way to everlasting life. Jesus says in Matthew 7:13–14, "Enter by the narrow gate. For the gate is wide and the way is easy that leads to destruction, and those who enter by it are many. For the gate is narrow and the way is hard that leads to life, and those who find it are few."

The wide gate of this world tells you that you are your own god. As the master of your domain in this alternate universe, the world applauds when you define your own truth. When the US Supreme Court redefines the biblical model of marriage between one man and one woman, Fortune 500 companies and media conglomerates alike will join in the celebration of the destruction of God's design for the family. Furthermore, the wide-gate worldview says you can undo what God has done. He creates life, but the laws of our land allow a mother to take the life of the child God created in her womb. Genesis 1:27 teaches us that God makes a person as either a male or a female. But our society's professional associations of medicine, education, and psychology espouse that God can make mistakes, and that those he created are wiser than him and can in effect determine their own gender. The wide gate of popular opinion and political correctness preaches its own version of equality, justice, and fairness. The narrow gate of God's truth, however, declares that God is the arbitrator of all truth claims.

In Matthew 7, Jesus declares further that those who embrace his truth will be like those who built their house on a solid foundation of rock. And those who reject his truth effectively build their houses on a foundation of shifting sand that will erode away during life's storms.

Next, Christians are commanded to put on the **breastplate of righteousness**. To be in right standing with a perfect, holy, and righteous God despite our wickedness is a solid wartime footing we don't deserve. The apostle Paul writes in 2 Corinthians 5:21, "For our sake he made him to be sin who knew no sin, so that in him we might become the righteousness of God." In the course of the daily battle for our allegiance, Satan constantly tries to entice us with all sorts of sinful thoughts, desires, and temptations. Yet our position in Christ helps keep us from falling into the enemy's trap if we will choose to live within the parameters God has established in his Word to protect us.

As part of God's battle plan, he has equipped his army of soldiers for Christ with **footwear** that advances the hope of the gospel into enemy territory. Isaiah 52:7 states,

> How beautiful upon the mountains
>> are the feet of him who brings good news,
> who publishes peace, who brings good news of happiness,
>> who publishes salvation,
>> who says to Zion, "Your God reigns."

My cleats were essential to my success as a baseball player. They provided my feet the stability I needed to accelerate and make quick turns in the outfield and on the base path. Without the cleated grip of the turf, I would have slipped and fallen repeatedly in my pursuit to catch the baseball, run out a single to first base, stretch a double into a triple, or steal a base to get into scoring position. Similarly, God has given me a passion and eagerness to share the life-giving, world-changing message of the gospel to those who are lost without the saving knowledge of Jesus Christ. Paul accurately describes this message as the "gospel of peace" because it heals broken hearts and calms the storms that turn our lives upside down.

In 2018 Americans ages thirty-five to forty-four were the highest spenders on footwear, spending an average of $531 annually.[4] I think it's safe to say we like our shoes. Just imagine if

Christians were equally ready to share their hope in Christ with those who have no hope.

Have you ever thought of faith in Christ as your **shield** to extinguish fiery arrows aimed in your direction? Did you catch that Paul wrote we should take up our shield of faith "in all circumstances"? That's one of the many reasons I suppose that Paul writes in 2 Corinthians 5:7, "For we walk by faith, not by sight." Faith sees what we can't. Faith knows what we don't. Faith conquers fear. And without faith, the Bible says, it's impossible to please God. But don't miss this, the shield of faith "can extinguish *all* the flaming darts of the evil one" (Ephesians 6:16, emphasis added). What Satan tries to camouflage or disguise, faith in Christ exposes with his light.

In contrast to the Christian's shield of faith, Paul describes how those without faith in Christ are defenseless against Satan's attacks in 2 Corinthians 4:3–5: "Even if our gospel is veiled, it is veiled to those who are perishing. In their case the god of this world has blinded the minds of the unbelievers, to keep them from seeing the light of the gospel of the glory of Christ, who is the image of God. For what we proclaim is not ourselves, but Jesus Christ as Lord, with ourselves as your servants for Jesus' sake."

Faith sees what we can't. Faith knows what we don't. Faith conquers fear.

When I think of the shield of faith, I'm again reminded of my brother in Christ and former Mets teammate Gary Carter. As our field general behind the plate, Gary led the charge by signaling to the pitcher exactly what pitch to throw. He was covered from head to toe with protective gear and sat in a crouched position while the pitcher hurled the baseball at him like a flaming dart. Meanwhile, the batter swung his bat just inches from Gary's head. And all the while, the joy of the Lord shone through Gary's smiling face and encouraging words. That's an image of the shield of faith that I'll never forget.

When I think of the **helmet of salvation** that Paul writes about, I'm reminded of the baseball helmet I put on every time before stepping up to home plate. I would never consider stepping into the batter's box without wearing that vital piece of safety equipment. It's certainly not the most stylish thing I've ever worn. But the batter's helmet truly is lifesaving gear when a baseball closes in on your head like a bullet. Comparing God's salvation from our sins through Jesus's sacrifice on the cross to a lifesaving helmet illustrates further how the mind is the battlefield for a person's heart. Please don't misunderstand me. I'm not suggesting that coming to faith in Christ is the result of someone's intellectual assent to the truth of the gospel. Scripture is clear that unless the Holy Spirit removes someone's spiritual blinders and convicts them of sin, repentance isn't possible. What I am saying, however, is that God created human beings with the capacity to reason and make decisions. And the god of this world knows that if he can deceive and delude someone into thinking they are their own god and in charge of their own lives, then that person will be well on their way through the wide gate that leads to eternal damnation in a place the Bible calls "hell."

Finally, the last weapon listed in Paul's description of the full armor of God is the **sword of the Spirit**, which is the Word of God. Throughout this book, we have unpacked the powerful promises of God's Word. The wonder and wisdom of God, witness of Christ's grace and gospel, and warning of God's judgment and mercy are all found in the Word of God. Without God's Word, I would have nothing to write about in this book. You certainly don't need a word from me. Oh, how we need God's Word every single day of our lives. The Holy Scriptures are more than sufficient for every problem we face in this world. The Bible has an answer for every dilemma and decision we need to make. The Bible doesn't just contain the Word of God. It *is* the Word of God—all sixty-six books—from Genesis through Revelation. Its timeless and universal truths are as relevant and applicable today as they were when they were written thousands of years ago. If Jesus—when Satan tempted him in the wilderness—quoted Scripture to resist the Enemy's attacks, how much more should we claim the authority of God's Word over the wisdom of this world? The Word of God is the only thing that will endure in this world. Isaiah 40:8 rightly declares, "The grass withers, the flower fades, but the word of our God will stand forever."

OUR LIFELINE

Did you notice that, having been fully equipped in the armor of God, the only time a soldier in God's army is vulnerable to spiritual attack by the enemy is when he or she turns their back on

God and retreats? Then and only then is their backside exposed. Why is this? Because God's battle plan is a one-way campaign through the narrow gate, aimed only at claiming enemy territory for the King of Kings and Lord of Lords. That's why Jesus promised in Matthew 16:18, "I will build my church, and the gates of hell shall not prevail against it."

Spiritual warfare is real. To deny the reality of its existence in the life of a Christian is to have already surrendered in defeat to the Enemy.

Prayer is essential for wartime footing. But make no mistake, spiritual warfare is not a physical battle of aggression. This war is fought on a Christian's knees, or whatever position you assume when you pray. After describing the whole armor of God, the apostle Paul lays out the battle plan in Ephesians 6:18: "Praying at all times in the Spirit, with all prayer and supplication. To that end, keep alert with all perseverance, making supplication for all the saints."

Prayer, Paul declares, is the game plan for defeating the enemy. He says further that the battle should be conducted through constant communication with Command Central—translation: "praying at all times." The word *supplication* is a form of prayer that means asking or begging humbly or earnestly on behalf of yourself or someone else.

In this biblical text, Paul encourages Christians to persevere in prayer. It's been said that "seeing is believing." But for the Christian who walks by faith and not by sight, *praying* is believing. The consistency and content of our prayers reveal volumes about what we believe about God. If we truly trust that God's heart is to help us and not hurt us, love us and not judge us, deliver us and not deny us, then why wouldn't we seek him in prayer for all our concerns and needs? Jesus promises that whatever someone asks in his name, he will answer. That doesn't mean we have a blank check with God. What it does mean is that whatever we pray according to God's will, he will grant. James 1:5–7 instructs us on how God answers prayers full of faith: "If any of you lacks wisdom, let him ask God, who gives generously to all without reproach, and it will be given him. But let him ask in faith, with no doubting, for the one who doubts is like a wave of the sea that is driven and tossed by the wind. For that person must not suppose that he will receive anything from the Lord."

Finally, Paul writes in Ephesians 6:18 that praying is the means by which one stays alert. As important as what you pray for is what you pray against. Since we know Satan is actively trying to destroy us, doesn't it make sense that we pray against his efforts? Furthermore, since we know the Enemy is a liar and deceiver, doesn't it behoove us to pray against his schemes? As we pray for God's protection from the Evil One and wisdom to avoid his deception, we should also pray against his advances.

There is something undeniable about the power of God's presence in prayer. At one of his lowest points in life, while hiding in a cave in fear for his life, the psalmist David prayed in Psalm 34:4–8,

I sought the LORD, and he answered me
    and delivered me from all my fears.
Those who look to him are radiant,
    and their faces shall never be ashamed.
This poor man cried, and the LORD heard him
    and saved him out of all his troubles.
The angel of the LORD encamps
    around those who fear him, and delivers them.

Oh, taste and see that the LORD is good!
    Blessed is the man who takes refuge in him!

Prayer allows us to take our focus off our circumstances and instead focus on God, who is in control of our situation. The apostle Paul taught in Scripture that prayer for the Christian should be an everyday expression of worship: "Rejoice always, pray without ceasing, give thanks in all circumstances; for this is the will of God in Christ Jesus for you" (1 Thessalonians 5:16–18).

Scripture teaches us to pray in faith with adoration, confession, and thanksgiving. In Philippians 4:6–7, Paul writes, "Do not be anxious about anything, but in everything by prayer and supplication with thanksgiving let your requests be made known to God. And the peace of God, which surpasses all understanding, will guard your hearts and your minds in Christ Jesus."

The next time you experience anxiety, stress, or fear, prayerfully thank God for the opportunity to exchange your frailties and insecurities for his peace. And then ask God to protect your heart and mind from the enemy's predictable attacks.

Shortly before Jesus's crucifixion, resurrection, and ascension to heaven, he prayed for protection from the Evil One—not for himself but for the disciples he had walked with on earth, as well as all the Christ-followers to come afterward, including our generation and all future generations: "I do not ask that you take them out of the world, but that you keep them from the evil one. They are not of the world, just as I am not of the world. Sanctify them in the truth; your word is truth. As you sent me into the world, so I have sent them into the world. And for their sake I consecrate myself, that they also may be sanctified in truth" (John 17:15–19).

> **Thank God for the opportunity to exchange your frailties and insecurities for his peace.**

Here Jesus is praying specifically for the eleven men he had spent about 70 percent of his time with during his ministry on earth. He doesn't pray for their deliverance from this world but instead for their perseverance in the faith as they lived in the world. To be in the world but not of the world is like a ship in the ocean that keeps the ocean out of the ship. Jesus knew his disciples would scatter in fear as he hung on the cross. Nevertheless, he prayed for their restoration and commissioned them to continue faithfully obeying and teaching God's truth—to be like salt that adds flavor to life and light that shows the way to life everlasting. Jesus knew that the same enemy who had tempted him in the wilderness would attack his disciples, raise up false teachers, and sow dissension. Jesus told them not to be afraid, because he was leaving them with a helper—the Holy Spirit. In other words, God in the flesh was leaving them God in the Spirit to indwell their hearts, minds, and bodies. Consequently, Jesus said, his followers, in the power of the Holy Spirit, would over the generations cumulatively do even greater things than he did during his three-year earthly ministry. "Truly, truly, I say to you, whoever believes in me will also do the works that I do; and greater works than these will he do, because I am going to the Father. Whatever you ask in my name, this I will do, that the Father may be glorified in the Son" (John 14:12–13).

Jesus promised his disciples that if they gave their hearts fully to the work of the Lord, he would answer their prayers for the glory of God. Their labor would not be in vain. Jesus said he would build his church, and as the Good Shepherd, he would always be the head of the church. But Jesus's prayer didn't stop there.

He prayed specifically for those who would trust in him from generation to generation. I'm overwhelmed just thinking that Jesus prayed for me before ascending to heaven to be with God the Father. He prayed for you too.

"I do not ask for these only, but also for those who will believe in me through their word, that they may all be one, just as you, Father, are in me, and I in you, that they also may be in us, so that the world may believe that you have sent me. The glory that you have given me I have given to them, that they may be one even as we are one, I in them and you in me, that they may become perfectly one, so that the world may know that you sent me and loved them even as you loved me" (John 17:20–23).

Did you ever consider that you could be the answer to Jesus's prayer for someone to know him as their Savior and Lord? When Jesus prayed that you would profess his name above every other name, he did so for your sake and the sake of others whom you would reach with the gospel. Jesus envisioned you as part of that great multitude praising God from every race, language, tribe, nation, and social class. He didn't pray for uniformity, but he did pray for unity so that everyone would know that "God so loved the world, that he gave his only Son, that whoever believes in him should not perish but have eternal life" (John 3:16).

And finally, Jesus concludes his prayer by asking God the Father that his followers be reunited with him in heaven. "Father, I desire that they also, whom you have given me, may be with me where I am, to see my glory that you have given me because you loved me before the foundation of the world. O righteous Father, even though the world does not know you, I know you, and these know that you have sent me. I made known to them your name, and I will continue to make it known, that the love with which you have loved me may be in them, and I in them" (John 17:24–26).

As Jesus faces the cross, he does so by praying victoriously that God's love will forevermore shine in the hearts of those who receive his love and forgiveness. Ironically, we exhaust a lot of time and energy praying people out of heaven. What I mean by this is that to pray for healing of a brother or sister in Christ this side of heaven is to ask for more time with them on this earth at the expense of delaying their eternal reward in the presence of Jesus. And while this is understandable, considering our great love for family and friends, how much more should we be praying for those among us who don't yet have the name of Jesus written on their hearts? May we recommit ourselves to praying more fervently that people would go to heaven when they die, just as we pray for those who are already going to heaven when they die.

In the Old Testament, in Jeremiah 29:11–14, God's Word promises us that when we seek him with all our heart, we will find him. When we call on God in prayer with humility and a longing for his will to be done in our lives, he never disappoints.

> I know the plans I have for you, declares the LORD, plans for welfare and not for evil, to give you a future and a hope. Then you will call upon me and come and pray to me, and I will hear you. You will seek me and find me, when you seek me with all your heart. I will be found by you, declares the LORD, and I will restore your fortunes and gather you from all the nations and all the places where I have driven you, declares the LORD, and I will bring you back to the place from which I sent you into exile.

In this passage, the Lord promised to rescue, redeem, and restore the Israelites after seventy years under Babylonian captivity. Now that's a long season to be out of your comfort zone.

Yet in the midst of the Israelites' exile, God's thoughts were always on his chosen people. His plans for good and not evil would not be thwarted by a pagan nation and enemy of God. God had preestablished a beginning and an end for the Israelites' season of suffering. He was always in control of the situation. Yet to the Israelites it may have seemed that King Nebuchadnezzar was calling the shots. Nevertheless, God never turned his back on his people. He was always working out his perfect plan. The Israelites' hope was found in the God of Abraham, Isaac, and Jacob. Yes, God chastened the Israelites for their rebellious, idolatrous ways. But God never broke the promise he made to Abraham to make a great nation, out of which would come the Savior of the world. And from the lineage of King David came the Messiah—Jesus Christ. And as Jesus lived on this earth, he who was sinless dwelled among sinners like Zacchaeus, a crooked tax collector. And when Zacchaeus repented of his sin, "Jesus said to him, 'Today salvation has come to this house, since he also is a son of Abraham. For the Son of Man came to seek and to save the lost'" (Luke 19:9–10).

Jesus is still seeking and saving the lost. I'm glad Jesus found me in my pit. If he can rescue, redeem, and restore a sinner like me, he can turn your season around too.

THINK ABOUT IT

1. What has the Father of Lies been whispering in your ear lately?
2. Consider the various parts of the armor of God—belt of truth, breastplate of righteousness, shoes as the gospel of peace, shield of faith, helmet of salvation, and sword of the Spirit. In which of those areas do you feel most prepared? And least?
3. In John 17:20–21, what did Jesus pray *for you*? How does that make you feel?
4. What did Jesus mean when he said his followers would do greater works than he did on earth?
5. On a scale of 1 (sporadic) to 5 (pray without ceasing), how would you rate your prayer life?
6. What have you been praying most about lately?
7. What people in your life aren't currently in your prayers but should be?

REJOICE ALWAYS

> Blessed be the God and Father of our Lord Jesus Christ! According to his great mercy, he has caused us to be born again to a living hope through the resurrection of Jesus Christ from the dead.

1 PETER 1:3

There is nothing quite like hearing a stadium-packed crowd erupt in applause while the public address speaker announces your name and you step up to home plate. Then with one swing of the bat, tens of thousands of people jump to their feet screaming and clapping as you take a home run trot around the bases. Those standing ovations never got old—not even after 335 home runs. To be honest, ever since my playing days in the big leagues—and even to this day—it's always felt a little weird that someone might be interested in my autograph. And although the attention is flattering, I've always found it extremely humbling at the same time. My mom ingrained in me from a young age that the ground is level at the cross and everybody is somebody. Maybe that's why my mom named me Darryl Eugene. Believe you me, with a name like that, you're not about to act too high and mighty—even if you can hit a baseball over five hundred feet. The fact of the matter is that human beings weren't created to be worshipped. No matter how many statues are erected, bronze busts are created, or baseball cards are printed, only One is worthy of all honor, glory, praise, and worship.

We read a majestic statement of praise in Philippians 2:9–10: "God has highly exalted him and bestowed on him the name that is above every name, so that at the name of Jesus every knee should bow, in heaven and on earth and under the earth." No number of World Series championships, victory parades through Times Square, or postgame champagne showers can rival the awesomeness of God's mighty works recorded throughout Scripture. He spoke the world into creation out of nothing. He raised up a tiny, inconspicuous nation of Israelites, from whom the Savior of the world came to deliver you and me from the condemnation of our sins. And he did this by exiting heaven and entering this world through the womb of a virgin. His perfect, sinless life then garnered him a criminal's death and burial in a rich man's tomb. What seemed to be humanity's most devastating defeat became a prelude to the greatest victory in the history of humankind. God brought Jesus back to life from the dead. "Blessed be the God and Father of our Lord Jesus Christ! According to his great mercy, he has caused us to be born again to a living hope through the resurrection of Jesus Christ from the dead" (1 Peter 1:3).

Death has been defeated forever. Because the tomb could not hold Jesus, for those of us who receive God's gift of forgiveness, our sins will not be held against us. When I accepted God's gift of grace in Jesus's salvation from my sins, I received new life in Jesus Christ. Hallelujah! I am born again!

A NEW ME

My identity has been redefined. I no longer see myself, my circumstances, or others in the same way. My mind has been renewed. I think differently and talk differently. The shame, guilt, and insecurities that shadowed me my entire life have been overcome by God's glorious light. My scars and pain have a purpose. I now can forgive myself and others. I seek to serve others instead of desiring to be served. No longer am I a slave to sin. I am God's choice servant. No longer am I God's enemy. I am his ambassador of reconciliation. I don't hunger and thirst anymore to be whole and complete. Instead of running from

Instead of running from God, I run to him every day in prayer. And now my running doesn't exhaust me.

God, I run to him every day in prayer. And now my running doesn't exhaust me. I don't grow weary and tired as I run God's race. My weakness is now a platform to display God's strength. He is the breath in my lungs, the love in my heart, and the purpose in my steps. As I daily read and meditate on God's Word, I learn how to love God more with all my heart, mind, soul, and strength.

All that to say, I've been changed. But this makeover will not fade away. The transformation is eternal. And yes, I'm still a work in progress. Jesus continues to refine me and remake me more in his likeness, pruning away the parts in my life that don't point others to him. And as I mature in my relationship with Jesus, I continue to learn and discover that the more I'm willing to let go of control of my life, the more he replaces my old, tired ways with his new and improved way of living a Christ-centered life.

To illustrate this daily reality in my life, I've taken the letters in my name to express how God's rescuing, redeeming, and restoring grace, mercy, and love continue to transform me from the inside out. Because of Christ in me, I have gone from:

Defeated to Delivered;
Addicted to Absolved;
Rejected to Redeemed;
Run down to Reborn;
Yearning to Yielded;
Lost to Loved;

Seeker to Saved;

Tempted to Triumphant;

Rebellious to Repentant;

Abdicated to Advocating;

Wasted to Washed by Jesus's blood;

Bitter to Better;

Ego-driven to Eternally minded;

Rebuked to Restored;

Reckless to Rescued;

Yo-yoed to Yoked in Christ.

Can you do the same with your name? Give it a try.

A JOYFUL NOISE

Whatever season of life you're in, the unchanging truth is that you and I can always rejoice, for God is good all the time. And all the time God is good. When I think about all that God has done as Father, Son, and Holy Spirit, I could talk, pray, and sing forever and never run out of superlatives, accolades, or words of praise and thankfulness for all the great things he has done throughout history and continues to do in my life today. King David, the psalmist, might be the most prolific writer ever of praise-worthy tributes to God. Psalm 100 is rich in its instruction and example of how to give God the praise and honor he is due.

Make a joyful noise to the LORD, all the earth!
    Serve the Lord with gladness!
    Come into his presence with singing!

Know that the LORD, he is God!
    It is he who made us, and we are his;
    we are his people, and the sheep of his pasture.

Enter his gates with thanksgiving,
    and his courts with praise!
    Give thanks to him; bless his name!

For the LORD is good;
    his steadfast love endures forever,
    and his faithfulness to all generations.

There is ample reason to celebrate and rejoice in God's goodness every day of our lives. How are you making a "joyful noise unto the Lord"? The world is a noisy place. Talking heads are everywhere you turn. Social media has amplified the voice of anyone with a digital device and Wi-Fi connection. While that is empowering, it can also be distracting. I have an Instagram account with more than fifty-two thousand followers.[1] If you follow me already, you know I use my social media platform to rejoice in the Lord and encourage others with God's Word. You can do the same.

Let your light shine, not on yourself but on Jesus. Bring

God glory with the videos, blogs, and posts you upload to social media. He is worthy of all praise all the time. But the Bible doesn't instruct us to praise God just with our voices. "Serve the Lord with gladness," the psalmist writes. The apostle Paul explains this idea clearly in Colossians 3:16–17: "Let the word of Christ dwell in you richly, teaching and admonishing one another in all wisdom, singing psalms and hymns and spiritual songs, with thankfulness in your hearts to God. And whatever you do, in word or deed, do everything in the name of the Lord Jesus, giving thanks to God the Father through him."

The Bible teaches us to filter everything we say or do by a single question: Am I rejoicing in Jesus? King David also reminds us in Psalm 100 that we owe a debt of gratitude to God because he made us. Is a heart of gratefulness for what Jesus has done in your life and mine too much to expect for the debt he paid to give you and me new life in him?

In Psalm 145:3–4, King David writes, "Great is the LORD, and greatly to be praised, and his greatness is unsearchable. One generation shall commend your works to another, and shall declare your mighty acts." Followers of Jesus Christ have the responsibility to make sure that the next generation knows what a mighty God we serve. How will they know if they don't see his transforming power in our lives? How will they understand the reason for our hope if we don't proclaim the unsearchable riches of God's Word? For if we do, the Bible promises that there will be those in the next generation who turn to faith in God as well.

"For 'everyone who calls on the name of the Lord will be

saved.' How then will they call on him in whom they have not believed? And how are they to believe in him of whom they have never heard? And how are they to hear without someone preaching? And how are they to preach unless they are sent? As it is written, 'How beautiful are the feet of those who preach the good news!'" (Romans 10:13–15).

This is why I do what I do. I have hung up my baseball cleats to tread another path, pointing as many people as possible through the Narrow Gate. Will you walk through it with me?

I pray that I will always be willing to go wherever, to share the love of Jesus with whomever, whenever the opportunity is available and at whatever the cost. Does that sound like an impossible task? Humanly speaking, it is. But Jesus said in Matthew 19:26, "With man this is impossible, but with God all things are possible."

THINK ABOUT IT

1. What does it mean to be born again?
2. How does Jesus's resurrection provide hope for us?
3. How can we rejoice in the Lord in bad times?
4. What do you think it means to bless God's name?
5. In what ways do you "serve the Lord with gladness" in your job, family, marriage, hobbies, community, and church?

6. How could you use social media to share your faith, without contributing to the chaos?

7. If you were to create a double acronym of your name, showing who you've been and who you are now in Christ, what would it be?

NOTES

1ST INNING: RECEIVE GOD'S GRACE
1. The full story is in my book *Straw: Finding My Way*, written with John Strausbaugh (Ecco, 2010).

3RD INNING: RENEW YOUR MIND
1. "State of the Bible 2019," American Bible Society, April 2019, https://www.americanbible.org/uploads/content/state-of-the -bible-2019_report_041619_final.pdf.
2. "Porn Stats," Covenant Eyes, 2018, http://www.covenanteyes .com/lemonade/wp-content/uploads/2013/02/covenant-eyes -porn-stats-2018-edition.pdf.

4TH INNING: REVEAL YOUR SCARS
1. "Americans Spent More than $16.5 Billion on Cosmetic Plastic Surgery in 2018," American Society of Plastic Surgeons, April 10, 2019.

5TH INNING: RELEASE GOD'S GRACE
1. Read more in *The Imperfect Marriage*, a book I wrote with my wife, Tracy (New York: Howard, 2014).

6TH INNING: REFLECT GOD'S HEART

1. "Hall of Famer Gary Carter Dies at 57," ESPN, February 16, 2012, https://www.espn.com/new-york/mlb/story /_/id/7583267/hall-fame-catcher-gary-carter-dies-age-57.

2. "Gary Carter Passes Away," *Fox News*, November 20, 2014, https://www.foxnews.com/sports/gary-carter-passes-away.

3. "Hall of Famer Gary Carter Dies at 57," ESPN, February 16, 2012, https://www.espn.com/new-york/mlb/story /_/id/7583267/hall-fame-catcher-gary-carter-dies-age-57.

4. "American Worldview Inventory 2020," Cultural Research Center, Arizona Christian University, https://www .arizonachristian.edu/culturalresearchcenter /americanworldviewinventory2020/, accessed July 2, 2020.

5. Billy Graham, "Answers," Billy Graham Evangelical Association, September 1, 2004, https://billygraham.org /answer/what-does-it-mean-to-be-poor-in-spirit-as-jesus-said -we-ought-to-be/.

6. Penn Jillette, "A Gift of a Bible," July 8, 2010, YouTube video, https://www.youtube.com/watch?v=6md638smQd8.

7TH INNING: RECLAIM GOD'S BEST

1. Brian Lokker, "1962 New York Mets: The Lovable Losers," How They Play, April 6, 2020, https://howtheyplay.com /team-sports/new-york-mets-first-season-1962.

2. Dictionary.com, s.v., "unalienable," https://www.dictionary .com/browse/unalienable?s=t.

3. "Abortion Rates by Country 2020," World Population Review, https://worldpopulationreview.com/countries/abortion-rates -by-country/, accessed July 2, 2020.

4. Number of Abortions—Abortion Counters, accessed June 15, 2020, http://www.numberofabortions.com/.

8TH INNING: RESTORE GOD'S PEACE

1. "Read MLB's Report on Its Investigation into Astros' Sign
   -Stealing," *Boston Globe*, January 13, 2020, https://www.boston
   .com/sports/boston-red-sox/2020/01/13/mlbs-report-astros
   -sign-stealing.
2. Ken Rosenthal and Evan Drellich, "The Astros Stole Signs
   Electronically in 2017—Part of a Much Broader Issue for
   Major League Baseball," *Athletic*, November 12, 2019, https://
   theathletic.com/1363451/2019/11/12/the-astros-stole
   -signs-electronically-in-2017-part-of-a-much-broader-issue
   -for-major-league-baseball/.
3. "Read MLB's Report," 2.
4. "Average Annual Consumer Expenditure on Footwear in
   the United States in 2018, by Age (in U.S. dollars)," Statista,
   November 20, 2019, https://www.statista.com/statistics/937094
   /average-annual-consumer-expenditure-on-footwear-by
   -age-us/.

9TH INNING: REJOICE ALWAYS

1. https://www.instagram.com/darrylstrawberry18.